DE HAVILLAND
VAMPIRE, VENOM AND SEA VIXEN

Above:
**The Venom FB4 had powered controls and a revised
fin and rudder shape.**

POSTWAR MILITARY AIRCRAFT:5

DE HAVILLAND
VAMPIRE, VENOM AND SEA VIXEN

PHILIP BIRTLES

LONDON

IAN ALLAN LTD

Contents

Previous page:

The FAW2 could carry four pods of unguided rockets on underwing pylons, instead of Red Top missiles. Underwing fuel tanks were carried outboard.
Royal Navy

First published 1986

ISBN 0 7110 1566 X

Published by Ian Allan Ltd, Shepperton, Surrey; and printed by Ian Allan Printing Ltd at their works at Coombelands in Runnymede, England

All photographs are de Havilland/Hawker Siddeley/ British Aerospace copyright unless otherwise credited.

1
Jet Engine Development

No account of de Havilland twin boom jet fighters would be complete without at first dealing with early de Havilland jet engine development.

The principle of the jet engine was well established before World War 2, and by 1939 Germany was undertaking its own research into the practical applications of this new form of aircraft propulsion, which anticipated far greater speeds than attainable with the highest performance piston engines. Britain, however, could not spare the time, materials, facilities or manpower to undertake any new research, relying on established production lines building Spitfires and Hurricane fighters and Merlin engines to attempt the seemingly impossible task of defending against a determined enemy during the Battle of Britain.

Only when the worst of this was barely over in early 1941, was it possible for Maj Frank Halford, the architect of de Havilland engines, to spare some effort for work on jet propulsion. The prewar de Havilland Engine Co had been geared up to producing a range of light piston engines, and production of the new turbine engines would require a great deal of reorganisation, with new tools, machines, materials and skills. The engine

company had been privately financed, but with the development of jet engines, government support would be required, as well as contracts for military production.

Jet propulsion would be most efficient and effective at speeds in excess of 500mph, and in early 1941 the aircraft designers could foresee the possibility of building aircraft to achieve this speed. A group of senior de Havilland personnel, including Sir Geoffrey de Havilland and Frank Halford, visited RAF Cranwell to see Sir Frank Whittle's pioneer work on the jet engine, and witnessed an early flight by the experimental Gloster E.28/39. The take-off run was very long and the flight duration very short, but it was a significant start, which demonstrated the possibility of a completely new era in flight.

In the early weeks of 1941 de Havilland was given the go-ahead to produce the new engine, and became the first British company to develop a jet

Below:
The Halford H.1 jet engine when developed led to the de Havilland Goblin, which was produced in large numbers for the Vampire.

Above:
During running on the test bed the Halford H.1 engine suffered some fire damage.

Above right:
The first Gloster Meteor to fly was DG206/G from Cranwell on 5 March 1943, powered by two Halford H.1 engines.

Right:
The Halford H.1 engines fitted in the Meteor nacelles with space to spare and were easily accessible.

engine for production, having been beaten in time by only Germany. No earlier attempts could have been made without risking defeat in the air by the Luftwaffe.

The engine layout chosen was the centrifugal type, which was easier to develop with less risk, but was less efficient, and had less development potential than the later axial type. The Halford H.1 engine, code-named 'Supercharger', and later named Goblin, pioneered practical jet development, and was therefore not the most efficient and refined design. Much experience had to be gained with materials and improvement in design. To achieve the best performance from these early power plants, a great deal of air had to be fed to the compressor, and the maximum thrust was achieved by having as short a jet pipe as possible to avoid loss of performance. The unusual twin boom configuration of the Vampire provided the means to achieve this, while keeping drag and weight to a minimum. Furthermore, the centrifugal engine featured a larger diameter than the axial flow jet, and high fuel consumption — particularly at low altitudes — kept the endurance of the aircraft short. Any way of keeping drag and weight to a minimum therefore gave the aircraft a better performance, justifying the installation of a jet engine. Also, without the instant power capability

of a piston engine driving a propeller, the early jet powered aircraft had a painfully slow acceleration, particularly on take-off, and so they required long runways. A fair proportion of the fuel carried was used during taxying.

Design of the Goblin engine commenced and the first drawings were issued to the shop floor on 8 August 1941. The project required a whole new approach to thermal, dynamic, mechanical and manufacturing considerations, the compressor and some of the other large components causing special problems.

On 13 April 1942, only 248 days from the issue of the first drawings, the prototype turbine engine was run on the Hatfield test-bed for the first time, with security ensured by posting armed guards

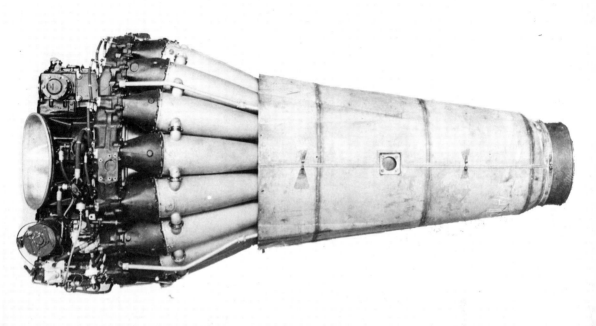

around the installation. Two days later a half-hour acceptance test run was made at half speed, and the following stripping down of the engine proved it to be fully satisfactory. The engine was re-assembled to begin its main programme of development running, its characteristic but unfamiliar whine being heard from the other side of the airfield. When questions were asked, the noise was attributed to a new electrical plant.

During running on 5 May, the engine went quiet as it came to a sudden stop. The intake had been sucked flat by the compressor, cutting off the air supply and stalling the engine. A complete strip revealed little damage and, following repair and re-assembly, it ran at full speed for the first time on 2 June, achieving its designed thrust within two months of its first run.

Towards the end of July de Havilland was investigating potential production arrangements, and on 10 September the company was asked to submit a complete detailed manufacturing plan, which it accomplished by 18 September. Eight days later a 25-hour flight approval run was completed, bringing total test bed running to nearly 20 hours on two engines, with others nearly completed.

The basic design of the Goblin remained largely unchanged during development, but a characteristic of gas turbine engines is that any minor improvements in efficiency have a relatively large effect on thrust. The major concentrations of effort in refining the design were on the combustion chambers (a new problem to the team of designers) and the engine compressor. New techniques of investigating vibration had to be evolved, one problem being to adhere strain gauges to the compressor blades at very high speeds.

However, all the problems were overcome, and within two years of the start of design work the Goblin engine was ready to fly. The aircraft company had been busy with Mosquito developments and the Hornet long range fighter, delaying progress on the Vampire airframe designed to take the new jet engine. The Gloster aircraft company had meanwhile followed the experimental E.28/39 with the twin jet Meteor single-seat day fighter, and its first prototype was ready to fly. Although

later aircraft were to be powered by a pair of Rolls-Royce Derwent jet engines, Goblin engines were installed and powered the maiden flight of the Meteor on 5 March 1943 flown by Michael Daunt, Gloster's chief test pilot.

Six months later the Vampire was ready with its single Goblin engine, and it made its maiden flight from Hatfield on 20 September, in the hands of Geoffrey de Havilland Jnr, son of the company's founder. The engines worked well and, although there was no hazard of a whirling propeller, the suction of the jet intakes were found to be enough to pull a man in, if he was unfortunate to be standing nearby.

With the Goblin now flying, de Havilland was instructed to send an example of the engine to the Lockheed Co in California, for installation in its XP-80A single-seat jet fighter. Unfortunately, the

Left:
Two Avro Lancastrians were used as flying test beds for the Ghost engines prior to their installation in the Comet airliner. Flying at the lower altitudes, the Lancastrians could cruise with their two Merlin engines shut down. *C. E. Brown*

Inset:
High altitude testing of the Ghost engine was undertaken in specially-modified Vampire TG278 fitted with a pressurised cabin and extended wing tips.

Below:
The Ghost engine for the Venom was similar in configuration to the Goblin, but had larger combustion chambers and developed more thrust.

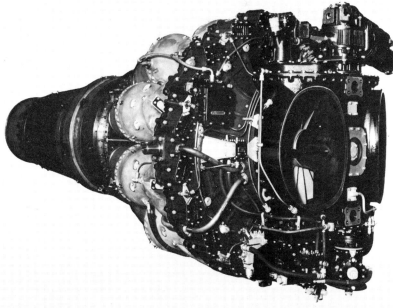

XP-80A's intake structure was not strong enough, and during ground runs it was sucked in, badly damaging the engine. A replacement engine was shipped out rapidly, allowing the XP-80A to fly for the first in January 1944. Both the Vampire and XP-80A easily exceeded 500mph in the spring of 1944, powered by the all-British Goblin jet engine.

The Air Ministry type approval tests were passed on 2 February 1945, the Goblin thus becoming the first jet engine to achieve this feat, and a new factory was starting deliveries of the production units. The prototype engines had a static thrust of 2,700lb, and by the end of the war, with a thrust of 3,100lb, the Goblin was the most powerful jet engine in production in Britain. Later versions of the Goblin developed 3,500lb of thrust.

Despite a relatively low effort, compared with Germany, de Havilland had built a lighter engine with a lower fuel consumption per pound of thrust. Also the standard of reliability was much higher, the typical BMW 003 axial flow engine needing an overhaul every 25 flying hours.

In July and August 1948 the Goblin had the most severe tests ever conducted on an aero-engine. It was run on the test bed over a period of seven weeks, giving the equivalent of 462 combat sorties each of 65 minutes duration. Maximum power was used for each for 1½ minutes to simulate take-off, and five minutes to represent combat. The engine still gave full power at the end of the test, and when stripped looked in such good condition that from January to March 1949 the test was repeated: it attained 1,000 hours between

overhaul, including 100 hours at full power, in representative operational conditions.

The Ghost engine for the later Venom was of similar design to the Goblin, benefiting from the growing experience which gave it 5,000lb thrust. Test bed running of the Ghost engine commenced just before VJ Day, and four years later it was powering the next generation of jet fighters. The Ghost was at that time the most powerful jet engine available and had a lower installed drag and weight than any other turbine powerplant.

Both the Goblin and Ghost engines were good examples of effective use of the design knowledge available at the time. The adoption of the relatively safe centrifugal design gave a reliable engine for world-wide service at an early date, while the more advanced layout of the axial type could be studied with less urgency. By choosing a single-sided, rather than double-sided compressor, the combined efficiency of the aircraft and power unit was greater. This was achieved by close collaboration between the engine and the aircraft divisions of de Havilland.

Simplicity of design was maintained in the Ghost by pioneering the straight-through flow of combustion gases, without any major changes of direction before reaching the turbine blades. The straightforward cantilever mounting and simple two bearing main shaft were examples of practical thinking at an early stage.

The Ghost engine was then redesigned to become the world's first jet engine certificated for civil flying when it was selected for the de Havilland Comet airliner. With some 80% of its components redesigned the 'civil' Ghost engine was awarded its type certificate on 28 June 1948, the first jet ever to be approved in the normal category for civil transport operation.

Below:
Vampire Mk 1 VV454 was fitted with a re-heat to a Ghost jet engine in the autumn of 1950. Before flight trials it was tested in a special ground rig.

2
Vampire Development and Production

Detail design of the de Havilland DH.100 Vampire commenced in early 1942 to Air Ministry Specification E.6/41. Although this specification called for an experimental prototype, provision was made for fitting four of the new 20mm Hispano cannons in the underside of the fuselage nacelle. Early in May 1942 permission was granted to proceed with construction of the jet fighter, but any production line for quantities of aircraft would have to be at somewhere other than Hatfield, because of the existing saturation of the manufacturing facilities there.

By September 1942 the mock-up was well advanced with a representative cockpit layout and many of the detail assemblies installed. To check the jet efflux clearance, the twin booms and tailplane had been mounted in a relative position on the engine test bed. Progress on the design was slow, however, because of the priority project work on major Mosquito developments, but when the jet fighter was given the priority it deserved, progress improved dramatically. This assured not only the future of the Vampire, but also gave an

application for the Goblin engine, which otherwise would have been lacking.

The official specification demanded a maximum speed of 490mph, together with a service ceiling of over 48,000ft. To achieve this performance using a new form of power, whilst carrying four guns with 150 rounds each, required an efficient design. As a result the Vampire was the last of the unsophisticated combat aircraft to be flown by RAF Fighter Command, combining Spitfire simplicity with jet performance.

Construction of three prototypes was undertaken in the experimental department at Hatfield, the smooth, streamlined fuselage nacelle being constructed in two halves from the familiar Mosquito-style plywood sandwich with balsa wood as a stabilising filling. Each half was equipped and joined along the centre line. The pilot was housed

Below:
The Vampire prototype, fitted with tall fins and rudders, made its first flight from the grass airfield at Hatfield, piloted by Geoffrey de Havilland Jnr.

under a forward-placed, rearward-sliding bubble canopy, without an ejector seat, but with an excellent all-round view. The fabric-covered wooden construction of the fuselage up to the engine bulkhead gave a very smooth finish. The wings, booms and tail were all of flush-riveted aluminium construction, and easy access was given to the engine by having removable cowlings on top and bottom, as well as an easily removable jet pipe. Simplicity was maintained by having all flying controls operated manually, without any power assistance, and no radar was fitted, the guns being aimed using a single gyro gunsight. As there was no need for propeller clearance, the tricycle undercarriage was kept short, making accessibility even easier. The only unconventional feature of the design was its very necessary twin-boom layout.

The Vampire, known initially by its code-name 'Spider Crab', took to the air from the grass surface of Hatfield Aerodrome 16 months after the go-ahead, and by early 1944 was exceeding 500mph by a handsome margin over a wide altitude range. This first prototype, LZ548/G, featured tall pointed rudders, but production Vampire F Mk 1s were to have a flat topped fins and rudders, later adopting the more familiar de Havilland shape in subsequent marks. The wings had an equal taper on the leading and trailing edges with provision for underwing jettisonable fuel tanks, and small flaps.

The second prototype, LZ551/G, soon joined the flight testing, and was followed by third and final prototype MP838/G on 13 May 1944. (The 'G' after the serial number signified the security aspects of the prototypes, which specified a guard on the aircraft at all times.) No provision was made for a development batch of Vampires for testing, much of the initial work being undertaken on the hand-built prototypes. The third aircraft was the first to be fitted with armament, consisting of four fixed 20mm Hispano cannon. A simple reflector gun sight was located on the instrument panel coaming.

Because Hatfield was fully committed to Mosquito production, an alternative factory with adequate capacity had to be found to build the initial production order for 120 Vampires, which was later increased to 300. The English Electric factories at Preston and Samlesbury were selected to produce the Vampire F Mk 1s, the first aircraft, TG274/G, making its maiden flight from Samlesbury on 20 April 1945. The first 16 production aircraft joined the flight development programme covering a wide range of testing at Hatfield, Samlesbury and the government establishments. The first prototype played no further part in the test programme when it was destroyed following an engine failure on take off from Hatfield on 23 July 1945. Fortunately de Havilland's test pilot, Geoffrey Pike, escaped without serious injury.

The second prototype was given a 4% increase in flap area, lengthened oleos and an arrester hook for deck landing trials on HMS *Ocean*. It became the first jet aircraft to land and take off from an aircraft carrier on 3 December 1945, flown by Capt Eric 'Winkle' Brown. Before flying on to the ship's deck, trials were made at Farnborough by flying into an arrester wire at various speeds and offset distances. As a result of a breakage, the hook supports were strengthened to reduce the hazards aboard ship. Further practice on land was conducted at RNAS Ford on 2 December, ready for the actual attempt the next day. Despite doubtful weather, 'Winkle' Brown located HMS *Ocean*, and the ship prepared for his first landing. The most demanding aspect of the approach was that a decision to abort the landing had to be made early, because of the slow acceleration of the early-standard Goblin engine. Once the aircraft was settled on the approach, the ship could be seen to be pitching and rolling rather more violently than anticipated. However, the batsman gave steady guidance, bringing the aircraft straight in to a gentle landing, despite the pitching stern of the ship hitting the tail-skids just before touch down.

The aircraft was soon refuelled and made an unassisted take-off which was so short that the aircraft was 20ft up when it passed the captain's lookout point on the bridge. On the fourth landing the larger flaps were damaged by the arrester wires, but by removing 4sq ft of area, the trials continued three days later.

Despite the success of these trials the Vampire did not enter combat service with the Fleet Air Arm, due partly to the poor acceleration of its engine if there was a need to overshoot on landing, and also because of its lack of endurance over a hostile sea where a number of approaches might be needed in poor weather. The Vampire was to see some Fleet Air Arm service, but as an advanced

This picture:
**Vampire Mk 2 TX807 was powered by a Rolls-Royce
Nene engine which required additional air intakes
behind the cockpit.**

trainer and for development work: more on that shortly.

Meanwhile the third prototype, MP838, powered by a 2,500lb thrust Halford H1A engine, was delivered to the Aeroplane & Armament Experimental Establishment (A&AEE) at Boscombe Down for handling trials in April 1944. In the report published on 1 June 1944, the overall impressions were favourable. The cockpit was considered comfortable, with easy access to the well-arranged controls and instruments. The pilot's view was generally good, but spoilt in some places by distortion, and the thick windscreen supports. Also amongst the credits were good control during high speed taxying, excellent aileron control, very low cockpit noise levels and high speed at low level. Criticisms included a poor rate of climb, slow acceleration — these characteristics a result of the engine being at an early stage in its development — and directional unsteadiness which interfered with its efficiency as a gun platform.

Soon after its maiden flight from Samlesbury, the first production aircraft, TG274, was delivered to the A&AEE for handling trials in June 1945. Power came from a 2,700lb thrust Goblin 1 engine, and the all-up weight of the aircraft was 8,610lb. The view from the cockpit was still criticised, and the slight increase in engine thrust did little to shorten the take-off run, which was long compared with piston-engined fighters. The aircraft appeared to leap into the air at 110mph IAS, while the best climbing speed was 220mph IAS. Nonetheless the aircraft was pleasant to fly and directional behaviour was an improvement over the third prototype.

The second production aircraft, TG275, was converted to the prototype F Mk 3 to specification F.3/47, powered by a 3,100lb thrust Goblin 2 engine. Internal fuel tankage was increased from 202 to 326gal and a pair of 100gal drop tanks could be carried under the wings. The tailplane and elevator were lowered between a pair of more shapely fins and rudders. This prototype first flew on 4 November 1946 and was allocated to the A&AEE for handling trials from August 1947 until the following February. Its assessment considered that the F Mk 3 did not meet the required standards of stability under some conditions, either with or without the drop tanks. The type was, however, cleared for service pending the evolution and incorporation of suitable modifications, providing that pilots were warned of the shortcomings, and that it was not flown in bad weather or at night.

TG276 was the first of four Vampires built as F Mk 2s to specification F.11/45, powered by a Rolls-Royce Nene engine developing 4,500lb of

Above:
DH.108 TG306 broke up and fell into the River Thames on 27 September 1946, killing Geoffrey de Havilland Jnr.

thrust. This aircraft first flew in March 1946 and was allocated to Rolls-Royce at Hucknall for engine development. TG276 was then delivered to France as the Mk 51 Mistral testbed, the French version of the Vampire. The Nene engine had a double-sided compressor, and therefore in the British version had additional air intakes on the top engine cowling. However, these extra intakes were removed by the French and the original wing root intake modified slightly.

The second F Mk 2 was TG279, which was allocated to the RAE Farnborough, but was destroyed in a crash near Newbury on 12 September 1945. It was followed by TG280, which first flew in July 1946 and like TG276 was delivered to Rolls-Royce at Hucknall for engine development. The fourth F Mk 2 was the out-of-sequence TX807, which was evaluated at the A&AEE in October 1947 before being despatched to Australia to become the prototype F.30, adopting the RAAF identity of A78-2. Prior to this, F1 TG431 had been allocated to the RAAF as a trainer with the identity A78-1.

TG277 was used for service evaluation, to check performance, operation and maintenance in squadron use, before being delivered to Cosford on 10 October 1952 as a maintenance airframe (7004M). TG278 was allocated for Ghost engine development, and was given a larger engine compartment, a mainly metal canopy over a pressurised cockpit, and extended wingtips. This test bed, which made its maiden flight on 8 May 1947, was used for high altitude development of the new de Havilland jet engine, and demonstrated its capability when John Cunningham took it up to 59,446ft on 23 March 1948, achieving a new altitude record. TG281 was used for nose section installation trials for the DH.108 in preparation for the high speed third prototype, while TG282 was used for Goblin engine development.

The DH.108 was a swept wing tail-less research aircraft built by adapting the Vampire fuselage nacelle, fitting 43° swept-back metal wings, and a swept fin and rudder mounted above an extended jet pipe. Designed and built to specification E.18/45, the aircraft was intended to investigate the behaviour of swept wings and to provide basic design data for the DH.106 Comet jet transport, and the DH.110 fighter. TG283 was the first of three DH.108s, and the maiden flight was from the long runway at RAF Woodbridge on 15 May 1946 — there was not a suitable runway at Hatfield. This initial prototype was designed for low speed research and, following company trials to investigate the aerodynamic characteristics of the swept wing, the aircraft was transferred to the RAE Farnborough in October 1948 for further research flying. Tests included stability, control and landing trials, and the fitting of a long stroke Sea Vampire undercarriage to allow landings at higher angles of attack at speeds as low as 95kt. These trials ceased abruptly when the aircraft crashed at Hartley Wintney, Hants, on 1 May 1950 during stalling tests, killing the pilot, Sqn Ldr Genders.

Vampire TG284 was used for armament development trials by de Havilland and the A&AEE at Boscombe Down, where it arrived on 28 September 1945. On completion of these trials it was flown to 33 MU at Lyneham on 4 July 1947, before delivery to France on 8 January 1950 as the first of many Vampires to enter service with the French Air Force.

Above:
The third and final DH.108, VW120, still used a Vampire fuselage, but was further modified for high speed research.

TG285 was exhibited at the SBAC show at Radlett in 1946, while TG286 was modified to F21 standard for the Royal Navy. This version was designed to test the feasibility of operating jet aircraft from catapults and landing on flexible decks without an undercarriage, to save weight and complexity. Initially, the aircraft was flown low and slow along the runway at Farnborough to check controllability, and in July 1947 work started on building the actual landing installation on the airfield. Tests were made — with Captain 'Winkle' Brown sitting in the cockpit — by dropping the Vampire from a crane on to the runway carpet from various heights to test the energy absorption of the surface. The carpet deck consisted of five layers of vulcanised rubber above three layers of fire hoses inflated to a low pressure. This construction had to withstand the climate and the close proximity of the hot aircraft jet pipe. The carpet deck was ready for operations to commence by the middle of December, but bad weather persisted until wind conditions were ideal on 29 December. Once airborne 'Winkle' Brown made a dummy run over the 'deck' to check that conditions were right, before settling down to the first landing. During the final stages of the approach the aircraft speed dropped too low, and despite an increase of power would not respond. The arrester hook hit the approach end of the deck, jamming up, followed by the rear of the tail-booms, restricting the elevators. The nose of the aircraft pitched down violently into the carpet, bouncing back up into the air. Brown opened up, but then found the elevators immovable, so throttled back to crash land on the grass beyond the flexible deck. He was unhurt, but the aircraft was badly damaged with split cockpit structure.

Following detailed investigations into low speed flying with the Vampire and also tests to avoid the

arrester hook jamming up, flexible-deck trials were ready to continue in March 1948. The next approach was aborted because of a sudden drop in wind speed, but a successful landing was made into a 12mph wind on 17 March. Tests continued through the spring and summer of 1948, reducing the necessary wind speeds to zero and finally landing with a tail wind. On some of these latter landings the arrester gear took much additional strain, the limit being 5.6G, when the hook was torn from the aircraft and catapulted backwards at high speed. Fortunately no one was in the way. A total of 40 flexible-deck landings were made by 'Winkle' Brown at Farnborough, often in front of interested VIPs, demonstrating the confidence built up in the experiments.

With the land-based part of the trials concluded successfully, sea trials of the flexible deck were ready to commence. These started aboard the light fleet carrier HMS *Warrior* on 3 November, using initially the prototype Vampire, LZ551, which had to be flown off the short carrier deck because it was not adapted for catapulting. The flexible deck was located on the rear half of the carrier's flight deck, painted with markings to assist the approach. The first approach at 118mph was slightly high because of the motion of the ship and turbulence over the roundown. The hook caught the wire and the aircraft was arrested on the carpet. Further landings followed; the fourth approach missed the wire, and the aircraft was flown around again. Minor damage was sustained throughout the programme, mainly caused by the wire supports being hit by the wingtips, but after modification the trials went smoothly, even on off-centre approaches and with cross-wind components. After the initial successes by 'Winkle' Brown, other pilots completed a number of successful landings, although one had to return to Lee-on-Solent when the hook claw broke mysteriously. The trials proved that it would be possible to provide landing grounds on board small ships or on land where insufficient facilities for runways existed, and to dispense with heavy aircraft undercarriages in the search for improved performance. However, such developments involved too fundamental a change in operating facilities; in particular the aircraft were far less easy to handle once on the ground.

Vampire F1 TG287 was used by English Electric as a trials aircraft, but eventually entered service with No 54 Squadron at Odiham in 1948. TG288 undertook service trials at the A&AEE, where it arrived on 4 November 1945, and was later delivered for service with the French Air Force in 1949. TG289 undertook aerodynamic testing of wingtip mounted cameras, before being allocated to maintenance training at Cosford in May 1953 as 7052M. The Empire Test Pilots' School (ETPS) used TG293 in 1946 before allocation to No 72 Squadron the next year. TG299 was used by the Aero Flight at Farnborough in 1946, eventually being allocated to Kirkham in November 1952 for ground instruction (7006M).

TG306 became the second DH.108 prototype intended for high speed research, hopefully to investigate speeds around Mach One. Sweepback of the wings was increased to 45° and power controls were provided. A 3,300lb thrust Goblin 3 powered the aircraft on its maiden flight from Hatfield on 23 August 1946, and level speeds were soon being attained in excess of 616mph, then the world's absolute speed record. Geoffrey de Havilland Jnr displayed the aerobatic capabilities of the aircraft at the SBAC show at Radlett on 12 and 13 September, before preparations were made for an attempt on the speed record over the official course along the south coast near Tangmere. He commenced practice flights for the record attempt, which were to be part of the routine high speed testing, and after waiting all day for calm air on 27 September, the conditions in the early evening appeared ideal for a practice high speed flight over the Thames Estuary. The aircraft was dived from 10,000ft to build up speed, and the plan was to fly at low level. However, 20 minutes after take-off the aircraft was seen to break up and fall into Egypt Bay near Gravesend killing the pilot. Much of the wreckage was recovered, including the engine, and as a result of the subsequent investigation it was assumed that the aircraft had flown through unexpected turbulence, which had

raised the Mach number and caused a violent pitch down of the nose. The wings then failed downwards with the sudden aerodynamic loads, although the aircraft was too low to recover anyway.

Despite this tragic loss, the brief flight trials had shown that a number of improvements were desirable. These included a lower pilot's seat, a redesigned canopy and a pointed nose. The third and final prototype, VW120, once again used a Vampire fuselage, but more extensively adapted for high speed research and powered by a 3,750lb thrust Goblin 4 engine. John Cunningham made the first flight from Hatfield on 24 July 1947, and after a year of steady development it was entered for an attempt on the 10km International Closed-Circuit speed record. Flown by John Derry on a course to the north of Hatfield in the evening of 12 April 1948, a new record of 605.23mph was achieved.

The high speed development flying continued with a gradual build up towards exceeding the speed of sound in a dive from high altitude. John Derry was the pilot on these hazardous tests, diving the aircraft from around 40,000ft to achieve the maximum speed. On 9 September he commenced the highest speed dive to date and completely lost control as the aircraft became the first to break the sound barrier in Britain. Despite all attempts to regain control the aircraft continued down, until the trim flaps were selected. The aircraft went into an inverted bunt and eventually stabilised in a gradual climb. The trim flaps were unlikely to have been significant in regaining control, the most likely reason being the raising of the speed of sound in the denser air at lower altitudes, taking this small low-powered aircraft out of the compressibility range. One further flight was made in excess of the speed of sound, but control was lost similarly and no further attempts were made.

Following the completion of the manufacturer's trials, the third DH.108 was delivered to the RAE at Farnborough to continue a programme of experimental flying. It, however, crashed in mysterious circumstances near Birkhill, Bucks, on 15 February 1950, killing the pilot, Sq Ldr Muller-Rowland. It was believed that control was lost when the pilot's oxygen system failed at high

altitude, as no fault could be found with the aircraft.

Minor development continued with various F Mk 1 Vampires, TG314 being the first to be fitted with the Goblin 2 engine and TG328 becoming the prototype F20 for the RN. TG336 was the first to feature cockpit pressurisation and TG343 was used for performance checking at the A&AEE in 1948, followed by wing fuel drop tank trials. TG372 was shipped to Canada for cold weather trials in 1946, where it remained to become part of the Canadian Museum collection at Rockcliff. TG426 was the second navalised

Vampire and was used for flexible-deck trials, but suffered undercarriage damage.

TG433 was the prototype FB6, an export version of the later RAF FB5 powered by a 3,300lb thrust Goblin 3 engine. TG433 was used for the later DH.108 canopy installation trials and also became a Goblin 3 engine test bed. The next aircraft off the production line had its wing span reduced to 38ft and made its first flight on 29 June 1948 for development of the FB Mk 5.

Following Vampire F1 production was the F Mk 3 to Spec F.3/47, commencing with VF335. Improvements included increasing tailplane chord

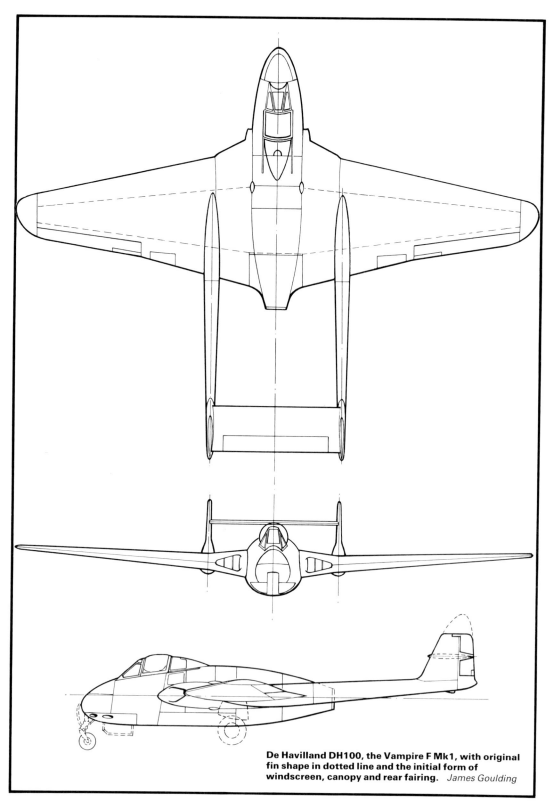

De Havilland DH100, the Vampire F Mk1, with original fin shape in dotted line and the initial form of windscreen, canopy and rear fairing. *James Goulding*

by 4.5in, reducing elevator chord by 1.5in and fitting streamlined fairings to the fin and lowered tailplane junction. The fin and rudder shape was changed to the more familiar curved de Havilland shape and range was increased by internal wing fuel tankage capable of carrying up to 326gal and provision for two 100 or 200gal underwing drop tanks. The F Mk 3 was first flown on 4 November 1946 and VF343 and VF345 were allocated to development and service trials. VG702 and VG703 were used for climatic and tropical trials over a 15month period in Singapore, the Philippines and Khartoum, ending in October 1949. These aircraft were used not only to assess flying performance in hot and high conditions, but also the effect of long periods of excess humidity and temperature on the structure and systems.

Amongst other aircraft converted to F21s for flexible-deck operations were VG701, VT802 and VT803.

Vampire F3 VV190 was used for Goblin 4 engine development in 1948 and gained second place in the Kemsley Trophy Race in July 1949, averaging 470mph. VV200 was also used by the de Havilland Engine Co for test flying.

Vampire F Mk 3 production was completed with VV213, and the next aircraft, VV214, was the first production FB Mk 5, making its maiden flight from Preston 23 June 1948. VV215 was delivered to Boscombe Down on 22 July for handling trials, and the next aircraft was used by both de Havilland and the A&AEE for performance measurement. VV217 was used for various tests, including the Sea Vixen nosewheel steering, VV454 had its Goblin engine fitted with an experimental reheat in an extended tail pipe in July 1950, whereas VV568 was only FB51, powered by a Rolls-Royce Nene engine, for

France. VV603 was allocated initially to the RAE Farnborough and also was on the charge of the Royal Radar Establishment, where it was delivered on 12 July 1951.

The two prototype Venoms, originally known as Vampire FB8s, were VV612 and VV613, taken from the Vampire allocations, but they will be dealt with in more detail in a later chapter.

Vampire FB5 VV675 was allocated for FB9 development on air conditioning trials for hot climates, and delivered to the A&AEE on 16 April 1951. VZ808 was the first de Havilland-built Vampire, being delivered from Hatfield to the A&AEE on 1 July 1949, but production continued for a while at Preston as well. One of the Hatfield-built FB5s, VZ835 was used for ejector seat installation development and spinning trials for the Vampire night fighter tailplane, starting in September 1950, and it subsequently went to Farnborough in January 1952. Only 33 Vampires were built at Hatfield, before the transfer of assembly to Chester, from where the first, VZ841, was delivered to No 501 Squadron at North Weald on 3 April 1951. Preston-built FB5 WA172 was used to test the DH.110 air intake shape.

Following the last FB5 WG847, off the English Electric production lines was the first production FB9 WG848, for operation in the Middle East and Asia. To overcome the high temperature problems, this tropical version was fitted with Godfrey refrigeration equipment in the wing root to supply cockpit air conditioning. Only one of this mark appears to have been used for development work, and this was WR249, delivered to No 19 MU at St Athan on 22 December 1953. A total of 1,565 Vampires had been built to RAF and RN order, many of which had been diverted to other air forces: in particular France acquired large numbers. Most of the production had been from Preston, but in addition to the 33 from Hatfield, 313 were built at Chester and the final eight were assembled by Fairey at Ringway. Furthermore, a considerable number were built for export: this production is covered in a later chapter.

3
The Vampire Enters Service

The Vampire entered service too late to participate in World War 2, initial deliveries being made to No 247 Squadron in April 1946 to commence the re-equipment of the Odiham wing with the new jet fighter. Sufficient Vampire Mk 1s were delivered to No 247 Squadron to allow participation in the Victory Day fly-past over London on 8 June 1946. In October 1946 both Nos 54 and 130 Squadrons commenced receiving Vampire F1s at Odiham, although at the end of January 1947 No 130 Squadron was renumbered No 72 Squadron. F1s remained in service with the Odiham wing until replaced with F3s during 1948, making some aircraft available for No 3 Squadron based at Wunstorf as the first unit in the 2nd Tactical Air Force (2TAF) to receive Vampires. The first arrived in April 1948 and were replaced by FB5s in May 1949, by which time the Squadron had moved to Gutersloh. Other surplus F1s were allocated to the Royal Auxiliary Air Force (RAuxAF), No 605 Squadron at Honiley becoming the first auxiliary squadron to be jet-equipped on 3 July 1948, later replacing the F1s with FB5s in March 1950. No 501 Squadron at Filton was the second auxiliary squadron to operate the jets, with F1s from February 1949 until converting to FB5s in 1952; No 502 Squadon at Aldergrove equipped in January 1951, converting to the FB5 in the same year, and subsequently became one of two auxiliary squadrons to fly the tropical FB9 — hardly appropriate in Northern Ireland.

A little-known use of Vampire F1s was with a number of the anti-aircraft co-operation units. No 595 Squadron was the first to be equipped in December 1946, flying from Fairwood Common and Pembrey in South Wales. It was renumbered No 5 Squadron in October 1948, and operated F3s at Chivenor from August 1950 until September 1951, still as an anti-aircraft co-operation unit.

No 631 Squadron commenced jet operations in the same role in August 1948 at Llanbedr, being renumbered No 20 Squadron in 1949, and continued with Vampires until October 1951.

The first major production version of the Vampire was the F3, which entered service initially at Odiham, its replacement with FB5s commencing in December 1949. In March 1950 No 72 Squadron moved to North Weald to receive its

FB5s, joining No 601 Squadron which had equipped with F3s the previous December. No 604 Squadron replaced its Spitfires with Vampire F3s in 1951, but North Weald squadrons replaced their Vampires with Meteors in 1952. The two squadrons remaining at Odiham began converting to Meteors, commencing with No 247 Squadron in May 1951 and No 54 Squadron in 1953. Meanwhile six Vampire F3s were the first jet fighters to fly across the Atlantic, when No 54 Squadron left Odiham and reached Goose Bay, via Iceland and Greenland, on 14 July 1948. They were escorted by a pair of 'met' Mosquitoes and participated in a number of displays and exercises in Canada and the USA, the highlight of the tour being the New York City centenary celebrations at the beginning of August.

Two further RAuxAF squadrons were equipped with Vampire F3s. No 608 Squadron flew the type at Middleton St George from 1950 until their replacement by FB5s in 1952, and No 614 Squadron operated its aircraft at Llandow from July 1950. FB5s were supplied to this squadron too as replacements in July 1952, and it later became the second auxiliary unit to operate FB9s.

Left:
Vampires first entered service in April 1946 when F1s equipped No 247 Squadron at RAF Odiham.
C. E. Brown

Above:
Vampire FB5s shared training duties with the T11, one of the units being No 5 FTS based at Oakington.
C. E. Brown

Bottom:
The first jet flight across the North Atlantic was by Vampires of No 54 Squadron: here the aircraft are taking off from their Odiham base.

The only other Vampire F3s to be operated by front-line RAF units were with No 73 Squadron, which equipped in October 1948 at Nicosia to become the first jet fighter squadron in the Middle East, and No 32 Squadron in May 1949. Both squadrons received FB5s and FB9s from 1951, No 32 Squadron also operating on two occasions from Shallufa and No 73 Squadron moving to Ta Kali and Habbaniya in Iraq. Both had ceased Vampire operations by the end of 1954.

Of the RAuxAF squadrons, those which were not re-equipped with Meteors continued with Vampire FB5s and some others were supplied with this mark as original jet equipment. The FB5 was produced in the largest numbers, combining fighter duties with an excellent ground attack capability. It served widely with the 2nd TAF in West Germany, in the Middle East, and even as far afield as Hong Kong. In 1950 No 602 Squadron received FB5s at Abbotsinch, and was followed during the next year by No 613 Squadron at Ringway in March, No 603 Squadron at Turnhouse in May, No 612 Squadron at Edzell in July and No 607 Squadron at Ouston. All the RAuxAF squadrons were disbanded by the Government in early 1957 as an economy measure.

In the 2nd TAF No 3 Squadron moved to Gutersloh with its Vampire F1s in June 1948, and No 16 Squadron at the same airfield exchanged its Tempests for Vampire FB5s in December 1948. The Gutersloh wing continued to build up its Vampire strength with the equipping of No 26 Squadron in April 1949, and No 71 Squadron replaced No 16 Squadron, which moved to Celle in November 1950. Meanwhile No 26 Squadron moved to Wunstorf in January 1950, receiving FB9s in mid-1952, and was later transferred to Oldenburg.

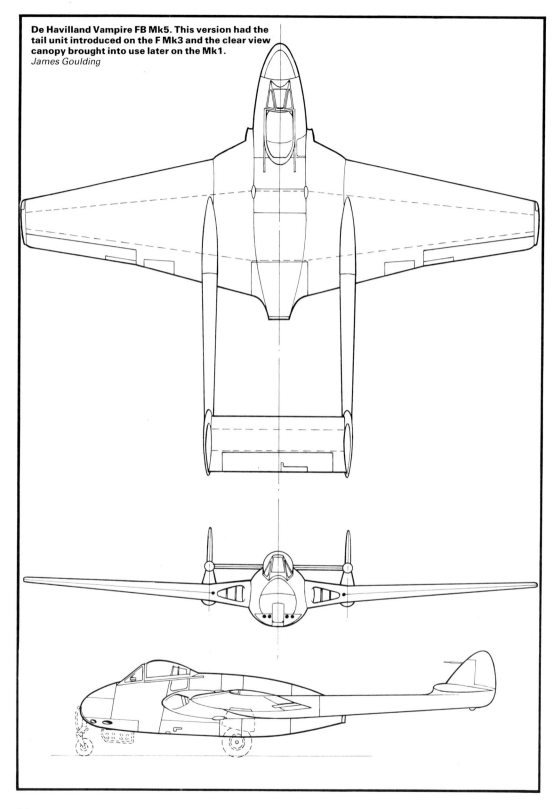

De Havilland Vampire FB Mk5. This version had the tail unit introduced on the F Mk3 and the clear view canopy brought into use later on the Mk1.
James Goulding

The next Vampire wing to equip with FB5s in 2TAF was at Wunstorf, commencing with No 4 Squadron in July 1950. This was joined by No 11 Squadron in the following month, No 5 Squadron in March 1952 and No 260 Squadron in July 1952. By 1953 No 4 Squadron had re-equipped with Sabres at Jever and the remaining three Vampire squadrons had re-equipped with Venoms.

In 1950 the Celle wing began receiving FB5s, commencing with No 14 Squadron which later moved to Fassberg. In November No 93 Squadron received FB5s, followed by No 94 Squadron the next year and No 145 Squadron the year after; they remained in operation until 1954. Fassberg was occupied by Nos 112 and 118 Squadrons from the spring of 1951, although both units were later based at Jever. No 234 Squadron equipped with FB5s and FB9s at Oldenburg in August 1952, later moving to Geilenkirchen, while No 67 Squadron used FB5s for six months at Wildenrath from September 1952, and No 130 Squadron again

became a Vampire operator for six months at Bruggen from August 1953.

Moving towards the warmer climates of the Middle East, No 185 Squadron began operating FB5s at Hal Far in Malta in September 1951, before moves were made to Luqa, Idris, Nicosia and finally Habbaniya, where the squadron was disbanded on 1 May 1953. No 6 Squadron received FB5s in October 1949 at Deversoir, later moving to Shaibah and Habbaniya. No 213 Squadron equipped with FB5s at Deversoir in December 1949, receiving FB9s in 1953 and finally disbanding

Below:
Vampires of No 54 Squadron and No 605 Auxiliary Squadron participated in the RAF display at Farnborough in July 1950.

Bottom:
No 604 Squadron Royal Auxiliary Air Force operated its Vampire F3s from North Weald for Exercise 'Emperor' in October 1950.

on 30 September 1954. Meanwhile No 249 Squadron equipped with FB5s in 1950 at Habbaniya and later moved to Deversoir. In June 1954 the Squadron began flying from Amman in Jordan and at the same time FB9s were supplied, until February of the next year.

In Asia, No 60 Squadron operated FB5s and later FB9s at Tengah from December 1950 until April 1955, and No 28 Squadron at Kai Tak with both fighter bomber versions from February 1951 until 1956. Both squadrons re-equipped with Venoms.

Three front-line RAF squadrons operated only Vampire FB9s, these being Nos 8, 20 and 45. No 8 Squadron flew them at Khormaksar, Aden from December 1952 to June 1955 when Venoms arrived; No 20 Squadron was at Oldenburg in 2nd TAF from 1952 until June 1954 when its aircraft were replaced by Sabres; and No 45 squadron operated FB9s with Meteors at Butterworth, Malaya, when its Hornets were replaced in March 1955. Seven months later Venoms were supplied.

Initially, operational training for the Vampire squadrons was handled by No 226 OCU at Pembrey and No 229 OCU at Chivenor, both being equipped with FB5s. Vampire FB5s were also used for advanced flying training, alongside Vampire trainers at Nos 1 FTS Linton-on-Ouse, 5 FTS at Oakington, 7 FTS (later to become 4 FTS) at Valley, and 8 FTS at Swinderby, as well as the RAF College at Cranwell. Armament training was undertaken by No 203 AFS at Driffield, and Nos 202 AFS and 2 APS at Acklington, co-ordinated by the Central Gunnery School (CGS) at Leconfield. Other training units to operate Vampire FB5s were the Central Fighter Establishment (CFE) at West Raynham, the Empire Test Pilots School (ETPS) at Farnborough, the RAF Flying College at Manby,

Top:
The Vampire FB Mk 5s could fire underwing-mounted rocket projectiles at ground targets. *Aeroplane*

Above:
FB5s, FB9s and T11s were used by No 7 FTS at Valley for advanced training. This line-up includes FB5s WA413, WA332 and WG843, FB9 WR194 and T11 XK624.

Right:
The initial Vampire F20s for the Fleet Air Arm were not fitted with arrester hooks. *C. E. Brown*

Inset:
A Sea Vampire F20 on approach to HMS *Vengeance* on 3 July 1950. *FAA Museum*

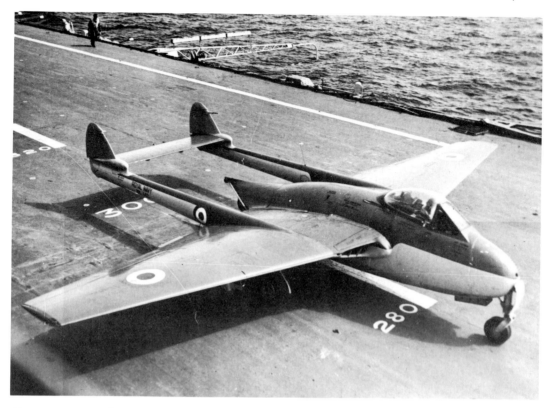

Above:
The Sea Vampire had a V-frame arrester hook stowed above the jet pipe. The compact size of the aircraft avoided the need for folding wings. *FAA Museum*

Above right:
Sea Vampire F21 VG701 was used for research into landings on flexible decks with the undercarriage retracted.

Below:
The second Vampire prototype, LZ551/G, was used by the RAE at Farnborough for flexible deck landing trials. *RAE Farnborough*

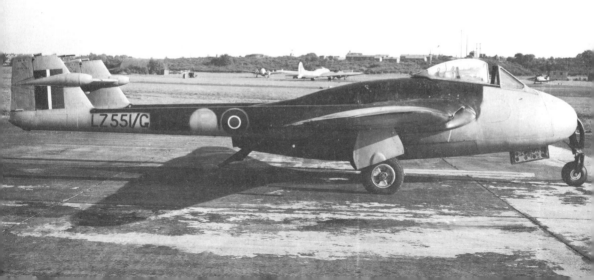

No 102 Flying Refresher School (FRS) at North Luffenham, and No 3 Civilian Anti Aircraft Co-operation Unit (CAACU) at Exeter until 1961.

No jet conversion trainer existed initially for introduction to flying the Vampire. Pilots were converting not only to a new type, but having only flown piston engined aircraft before, they had to master the new jet principles. The transition from one to another was achieved by a briefing on the new handling techniques and a familiarisation with the cockpit, with emphasis on the new controls. The low ground clearance resulting from the lack of a propeller, and the nose wheel undercarriage, helped with handling on the ground and visibility. Acceleration was far slower with the early low thrust jet engines, and controllability at low speeds was not assisted by the familiar propeller slipstream. The Vampire was, however, pleasant to fly and very much less demanding than many of the contemporary high performance propeller-driven aircraft, which were optimised for the highest possible top speed and had less than desirable characteristics at low speeds. The Vampire's clean, efficient design made it an effective interceptor, and the provision of wing hard points for bombs and rockets gave it a very valuable ground-attack capability, the cannon too being useful for keeping the enemies' heads down! The fighter-bomber role had already been antici-pated by de Havilland, but, with the selection of the more complex twin-engined Meteor as a standard RAF interceptor, the stable and straight-forward Vampire was allocated to ground attack duties throughout 2 TAF, the Middle East and Asia. In European theatres in wartime the Vampire would be used to harass enemy movements, with its effective reconnaissance and strike capability, while still being an accomplished interceptor able to maintain air superiority.

In the Middle East and Asia the aircraft trained for similar duties, but was rather more active in Malaya against the terrorists, bridging the gap between the long-range Hornets and the later Venoms with their improved performance. No 8 Squadron also provided support during the Mau Mau uprising in Kenya.

Single-seat Vampires continued serving with training units, later alongside the Vampire T11s, for some years after the type was withdrawn from front-line service, providing useful training experi-ence as an introduction to the Hawker Hunter.

With the success of the deck trials using the second prototype Vampire, an order was placed for six Sea Vampire development aircraft and 30 production versions, known as the Sea Vampire F Mk 20. An arrester hook was fitted above the jet pipe and the small overall dimensions of the aircraft avoided the heavy, expensive and compli-cated fitting of wing folding mechanism. With their relatively low endurance the Vampires were not intended for regular deck operations, but provided a cost effective introduction to jet flying for the naval aviators. The Vampire F20 was based on the RAF Mk 3, and the first public appearance of this naval version was at Yeovilton on 6 September 1947. Sea Vampires of the Carrier Trials Unit were based on HMS *Illustrious* in early December 1948, during Exercise 'Sunset' in the North Atlantic, when they were used for the first time as carrier-borne interceptors, and over 200 deck landings were made. A small detachment also served aboard HMS *Vengeance* in 1950. A single Sea Vampire F20, flown by Rear Adm Couchman, led the fly-past of over 300 FAA aircraft during the Queen's Review of the Royal Navy at Lee-on-Solent on 13 June 1953.

The production aircraft were issued to 700 Squa-dron at Ford, 702 Squadron at Culdrose and 787 Squadron. They were withdrawn from service in 1957, and the majority were scrapped at Lossie-mouth. The other naval conversion was the F21 used for flexible-deck trials, and although it did not enter service in the configuration intended, two saw service later with 764 Squadron.

4
Vampires for Export

The Vampire also achieved considerable export success, becoming the standard day fighter and ground attack aircraft with many air forces throughout the world. In addition to production from Britain, in some cases orders were large enough to justify licence production in the country concerned.

The first large export order for the British aircraft industry was placed on 9 February 1946 when de Havilland completed the negotiation of three contracts with the Swedish Government for the supply of Vampire fighters and Goblin engines, and the eventual licence production of Goblin 3 engines. On 4 June 1946 the first five Vampires, designated J28 for the Royal Swedish Air Force, left Hatfield on their delivery flight to Barkarby. The Vampires replaced Mustangs in Swedish service and operated with great success even within the Arctic Circle. The initial order was completed 15 months from the first delivery and a further batch was ordered on 22 January 1948, bringing the overall total to 70 aircraft. The Vampires introduced jet aircraft to a number of day fighter wings, the first unit being F.13 at Norrköping. The training of new pilots went without difficulty and exercises were held at Luleá, the base of F.21 well up into the Arctic Circle, where temperatures went as low as −45°C and where it was dark continuously from 4 December until 9 January. A final order for 200 Vampires was placed in 1948, to include a number of Vampire trainers. The single-seat Vampires remained in front-line service until 1958, some remaining for advanced training with F.5 Wing at Ljungbyhed.

The next order was an important one from Switzerland, initially for an evaluation batch of four F1s, the first being delivered to Geneva on 27 July 1946. The evaluation continued for a year under typical operating conditions, resulting in an order for 75 Vampires, similar to the FB5s but known as the export FB Mk 6s, powered by the 3,300lb thrust Goblin 3 engine. Following the initial production batch of 75 aircraft from the UK, licence production of 100 Swiss-built aircraft commenced at the Federal Aircraft Factory at Emmen and Pilatus at Stans. All the engines were

supplied from Britain and three more Vampires were assembled from spares at Emmen in 1960.

The first Commonwealth order was from the Royal Canadian Air Force (RCAF) in March 1947 for 85 F Mk 3s to be built in Britain, and assembled by de Havilland Canada. The first aircraft was demonstrated at Rockcliff near Ottawa in March 1948, with the first regular squadrons being formed at Trenton, followed by auxiliary squadrons at Montreal, Toronto, Winnipeg and Vancouver. No 410 Squadron formed an aerobatic team of six aircraft in 1949, demonstrating in Canada and the USA. The Vampires worked well in temperatures down to −60°F, an example being 12 Vampires with No 410 'Cougar' Squadron which operated in the Yukon on a winter exercise. The RCAF Vampires were withdrawn in the early 1950s, some being acquired by private owners as sports aircraft. Twelve ex-RCAF Vampires were purchased by Dominica, to add to 25 ex-Swedish Vampires, and 15 ex-RCAF Vampires were used to form Mexico's first jet fighter squadron.

In the spring of 1947 plans to license-build the Vampire for the Royal Australian Air Force (RAAF) were announced, the first example, powered by a 5,000lb thrust Rolls-Royce Nene engine, making its maiden flight from Bankstown, Sydney on 29 June 1949. Known as the F.30 with the RAAF, a total of 57 was built to replace Mustangs in the regular and citizens' air force

squadrons. These were followed by 23 FB Mk 31s, which remained in service with the regular squadrons until replaced by Sabres in 1955. Four out of five of the citizens' squadrons retained their Vampires, until they too were disbanded, in 1957.

Like the Swiss, Norway ordered a trial batch of four Vampires in the spring of 1948. These were taken from RAF stocks to speed delivery, the first three arriving at Gardemoen near Oslo on 29 April. As a result of the evaluation 25 FB5s were ordered for No 336 Squadron.

India purchased an initial batch of 39 F3s and FB52s from the de Havilland production lines, the first three being delivered to Cawnpore on 6 November 1948. Hindustan Aeronautics at Bangalore then commenced licence manufacture, building 247 single-seaters as well as some Vampire trainers for the Indian Air Force and Navy, before completion of the last aircraft in 1959.

A major user of the Vampire was the French Government, which was in urgent need of suitable combat aircraft to build up its depleted postwar air force. The Vampire proved ideal for the task, and the agreement including licence production and development by SNCA Sud-Est was reached in the spring of 1949. While production plans were being made some 76 Mk 5s were supplied from RAF stocks, and the initial licence-built version known as the FB Mk 51 made its maiden flight from Marignane on 27 January 1950. The production lines maintained a high rate from the start, because de Havilland supplied major assemblies initially, followed by unequipped components, and finally detailed parts, until full licence production was established. This resulted in a production rate of 10 aircraft per month only seven months after the first delivery. The Rolls-Royce Nene engine was already in production in France, and it was decided to adapt the Vampire to this power plant. Improvements were made to the original de Havilland-designed Mk 2 by deleting the extra air intakes on top of the fuselage and refining the

35

wing-root intakes. Further development by SNCASE left only the forward fuselage, the tail booms and tailplane common to the British version, the new 'Mistral' also having an ejector seat. The first production Mistral made its maiden flight at the end of 1951, achieving a maximum speed at sea level of 578mph, 50mph faster than the standard Mk 5. A total of 183 Vampires and 250 Mistrals were produced under licence in France, replacing F-47Ds with *4e Escadre* in 1951, followed by *3e, 5e* and *7e Escadres*, until Ouragons began to enter service in 1954.

South Africa ordered a squadron of 10 Mk 5s in early 1949. The aircraft were shipped from Britain, and the first example made its maiden flight after re-assembly on 8 February 1950. A further 40 Vampires were ordered, including FB9s, to replace SAAF Spitfires. They remained in front-line service and with the Active Citizen

Left:
France adapted the Vampire to take the Rolls-Royce Nene engine and with a number of other modifications it became known as the Mistral. *SNCASE*

Below left:
Two South African Air Force FB5s fly past Table Mountain. The SAAF placed an order for a squadron of Vampire FB5s before ordering further Mk 5s and Mk 9s.

Below:
Aeronautica Macchi built Vampires under licence for the Italian Air Force. *Macchi*

Force until replaced by Sabres in 1956, when many were allocated to advanced training.

The Italian Air Force standardised on the Vampire as a day fighter, placing an initial order on 29 November 1949, followed by a second one a year later. The first five ex-RAF aircraft were delivered for evaluation in early 1950, to allow experience with the aircraft to be built up while plans were made for licence production by Fiat, Alfa Romeo, Aeronautica Macchi and SAI Ambrosini for both the airframe and the engines. Two years after signing the agreement the British-supplied Vampires were operational, and the first of 80 licence-built aircraft had made its maiden flight on 18 December 1951, from the Macchi factory at Venegano near Milan. The Vampires equipped *4a Aerobrigata* and *20 Stormo*, and the mid-1950s were used for advanced training.

The first Middle Eastern order came from Egypt at the end of 1949, to re-equip its air force after the 1948 war with Israel. Before the aircraft could be delivered, the British Government placed an embargo on military sales to Egypt, but this was overcome by the acquisition of 30 FB52s from Italy via Syria. Following the lifting of the embargo in August 1953 a small batch was supplied from the UK. When the RAF withdrew from the Canal Zone in October 1954, the Egyptian Air Force took over the defensive role with 49 Vampires equipping four fighter-bomber squadrons. Vampires and MiG-15s were used for the defence of the Sinai in the October 1956 war with Israel,

Above left:
The Egyptian Air Force Vampire order was embargoed by the British Government, and early aircraft were acquired from Italy.

Left:
The only South American operator of Vampires was Venezuela which took delivery of its first aircraft in December 1952. Here 3B35, to FB5 standard, is surrounded by typical Venezuelan terrain.

Top:
Royal New Zealand Air Force FB5 NZ5731. A number of Vampires were ordered by the RNZAF and remained in service until 1972. *RNZAF*

Above:
The first three of six Vampires for Finland were delivered from Hatfield in January 1953.

the first Vampire being shot down on 31 October. At least three more were shot down and many more were destroyed on the ground by the Anglo-French operations in early November. Four of the survivors were presented to Saudi Arabia in July 1957, and seven were supplied to Jordan in October 1956 to add to the 10 FB9s presented by the RAF in December 1955, as the country's first jet combat aircraft.

The only sale to a South American customer was for 15 shipped out to Venezuela, the first flying on 22 December 1949 after re-assembly at Caracas. A further batch of FB5s was ordered in 1950 for *Escuadron de Cuza No 35* formed at Boca de Rio on 10 December 1952. The accident rate was high as only 10 Vampires had survived by 1959.

New Zealand ordered 18 Vampire FB Mk 52s in 1950, as the first jets in the Dominion, the aircraft being shipped out and assembled at Hobsonville. No 14 Squadron re-equipped with the Vampires on 3 September 1951, at its Ohakea base. This was one of only four airfields with paved runways, but the aircraft were also well suited to the grass airfields, which often had difficult approaches. No 14 Squadron was moved to Cyprus to strengthen the allied presence in the Middle East, flying Vampires leased from the RAF, their original aircraft passing to the home-based No 75 Squadron. In late 1952 a further eight ex-RAF FB5s were supplied to cover attrition and provide some stock for further years, and at the end of 1955 a further 20 Mk 5s were orderd. They remained in service with No 14 Squadron (which returned to New Zealand), No 75 Squadron, and the Fighter Operational Conversion Unit, until final retirement at the end of 1972.

The remaining overseas orders were for small numbers for customers in Europe, the Middle East and Africa. Finland ordered six Mk 52s, the first three being delivered on 22 January 1953 to Pori near Helsinki, where one is preserved following retirement in 1965. The Royal Iraqi Air Force ordered 12 Vampires in 1953 to equip No 5 Squadron at Rashid, its first jet fighter unit; later the same year the Lebanon ordered five Mk 52s, the first being delivered to Kleyate on 22 October 1953. The last Vampire export order came from southern Rhodesia for 24 FB9s for delivery between December 1953 and November 1955 to equip two squadrons.

Now all the single-seat Vampires have been retired apart from a small number flying in Switzerland on training and target towing duties.

5
The Vampire Night Fighter

The DH.113 Vampire night fighter was produced as a company-funded private venture design to provide a cost-effective export night fighter. Geoffrey Pike took the prototype on its maiden flight from Hatfield on 28 August 1949, power coming from a 3,350lb thrust Goblin 3 engine. The major difference from the single-seat Vampire was an enlarged fuselage nacelle to accommodate the somewhat ancient AI Mk10 radar, two crew and the additional equipment. The standard four 20mm cannon were retained and provision was made for a pair of 100gal drop tanks to be carried under the wings.

The first public appearance of the first of two prototypes was at the SBAC show at Farnborough only a few days after the initial flight, and the following month Egypt placed an order for 12. However, the British Government embargoed arms to Egypt and the aircraft were adopted by the RAF as the Vampire NF10, an interim aircraft pending the delivery of the more sophisticated Meteor and Venom night fighters.

The second prototype became part of the RAF allocation, the first real production aircraft, WP232, making its maiden flight from Hatfield on 19 February 1951 for delivery to the A&AEE on 30 March. WP236 was operated by the Handling Squadron at Manby for the compilation of pilots' notes, and WP240 was evaluated at Boscombe Down. Aircraft used for research included WP240 to test the Sea Vixen radome shape in 1955 and WP250 by Handley Page for boundary layer suction laminar flow wing section development from 1953 to 1956.

The first RAF unit to receive Vampire NF10s was No 25 Squadron at West Malling in July 1951, replacing its Mosquito NF36s. The Squadron worked up to operational service during the rest of the year, with No 151 Squadron at Leuchars on 15 September and No 23 Squadron at Coltishall in the same month also receiving NF10s.

For safety reasons if was desirable for the RAF to operate twin-engined night fighters, but with late deliveries of the Meteor night fighters, the Vampires filled an urgent gap. They did not have ejector seats for the crew, but despite having a poorer performance, as compared with the twin-engined Meteor, the Vampire night fighter had a greater endurance and was a better gun platform.

Although being home based, No 23 Squadron detached five aircraft to Fassberg in Germany for Exercise 'Hold Fast' in September 1952. The same

Below:
The private venture Vampire night fighter prototype G-5-2 flew with modified fins to balance the increased nose length.

unit flew 12 of its aircraft in the Queen's Review of the RAF at Odiham on 15 July 1953, four months before the replacement with Venoms began. In April 1954 Meteor night fighters began to replace the Vampires with both Nos 25 and 151 Squadrons, leaving 25 unused aircraft still held in storage at maintenance units.

Some of the aircraft were retained by the RAF for navigator training, the AI radar being removed and replaced by navigation equipment such as Rebecca 3 and Gee 3. The armament was retained to help maintain the centre of gravity and a new cockpit canopy was fitted to provide a better view and easier escape in an emergency. Ejector seats were still not fitted.

No 2 Air Navigation School (2 ANS) at Thorney Island was the first to receive these revised

Above left:
The RAF production standard Vampire NF10 returned to the traditional fin shape, but had tail plane extensions. Many of the RAF aircraft (like WM659 shown) were exported to India. *MoS*

Left:
NF10s were used by the RAF as interim night fighters, No 25 Squadron based at West Malling being one of the units. This is the fourth production NF10, WP235, under preparation for a night execise in December 1951.

Below left:
The Italian Air Force ordered 14 Vampire NF54s, the first, 3-167, being delivered in June 1951.

Below:
The Indian Air Force acquired 30 ex-RAF Vampire night fighters, which were refurbished at Chester before delivery.

Vampires in August 1955, eventually totalling around 14 aircraft with a pair of T11s for continuation training. Nearly two years later, in March 1957, No 1 ANS was re-formed at Topcliffe with nine Vampires sharing the training with Valettas and Marathons. The jet navigation courses lasted until 1959, when No 1 ANS discontinued them early in the year, followed by No 2 ANS in April. The aircraft were soon scrapped, apart from WP255 which flew as a hack with No 27 MU until the end of 1959. Some Vampire NF10s were used by the Central Navigation & Control School (CNCS) at Shawbury from May 1954 until September 1959 for the training of air traffic controllers.

The surplus aircraft not used by the RAF were offered for export after overhaul at the Chester factory. Italy ordered 14 new NF54s as interim all-weather fighters and for advanced night fighter training, which were delivered between 4 June 1951 and 25 March 1953. Switzerland ordered one new Vampire night fighter, U-1301, which was delivered on 1 January 1951. It was used for the testing of system and equipment in the Swiss licence-built Venoms, and later used for electronic countermeasures trials. Following its handover to the Swiss Air Force, it was flown on various evaluation tasks, before being withdrawn from service and scrapped at Emmen in 1961, because of the lack of ejector seats. The largest overseas sale was to India, which ordered 30 ex-RAF aircraft, modified to NF52s and delivered between 18 April and 15 October 1954.

Out of the 94 Vampire NF10s built, two now remain, one preserved in Italy and the other in India.

6
The Vampire Trainer

The Vampire trainer was an uncomplicated adaptation of the Vampire night fighter, by removing the AI radar from the nose and fitting dual controls in the side-by-side cockpit. Instead of having a radome in the nose, the front fuselage incorporated an upward opening large fairing hinged at the rear, where the aircraft batteries and communications equipment was located on an easily accessible shelf. As with the earlier Vampire family, the wooden fuselage was attached to the standard metal wings and tail booms, power coming from a 3,350lb thrust Goblin 3 engine. First announced publicly in August 1950, the private venture prototype, marked G-5-7, was shown at the SBAC display at Farnborough the following month. Despite looking complete externally, the aircraft had not flown, and was shown statically.

The purpose of the type was to provide the widest range of training duties possible, from advanced jet training through gunnery and weapons training, whilst having as much commonality as possible with the other Vampires. Two or four 20mm cannon could be installed under the fuselage, not only to provide realistic training but also to give the aircraft an operational capability. A standard reflector gunsight was fitted in the cockpit. Strong points were retained in the wings for the carriage of a pair of 1,000lb bombs, eight rockets or long range fuel tanks.

The Vampire trainer was originally built as a private venture but was intended to meet the RAF advanced trainer requirements. The prototype, G-5-7, featured the original Vampire tail with no outboard tail-plane extensions.

Early production Vampire T Mk 11s, featuring the old canopy, no ejector seats and the early fin shape, entered service with No 202 Advanced Flying School at Valley.

The Vampire trainer had full dual controls including a pair of reflector gun sights for weapons training.

The prototype featured the old night fighter framed canopy with an upward opening lid, and the fin and rudder were the traditional shape, but the outboard tailplane extensions were removed and bullet fairings were located on the fin-to-boom join. First flight was made from the grass airfield at Christchurch by John Wilson on 15 November 1950, for 25 minutes. Following company flight trials, the prototype became WW456 for official trials. It underwent service evaluation at No 204 AFS and then the CGS at Leconfield before adoption by the RAF as the Vampire T Mk 11, the trials being completed on 26 April 1951. The prototype was then delivered to A&AEE Boscombe Down on 29 April 1952 for further official trials.

Two pre-production aircraft, WW458 and WW461, came off the production line next at Christchurch, the first one flying on 1 December 1951 and being delivered to RNAS Culham on 21 January 1952 for evaluation by the RN. The second pre-production aircraft joined the first at RNAS Culham on 22 May, the successful trials resulting in orders for the Fleet Air Arm for the type as the T Mk 22.

Production for the RAF commenced at Christchurch with WZ414, which first flew on 19 January 1952, the first of 26 aircraft built at the factory before transfer of the main production to Chester. WZ414 was used for company trials before allocation to the ETPS. WZ415 and WZ417 were delivered to the A&AEE, and WZ419, which first flew on 27 March 1952, was allocated to development of the improved fin shape with a dorsal fairing, clear view upward opening canopy and the installation of ejector seats. The outboard tailplane extensions had already replaced the prototype bullet fairings. WZ419 first flew after modification on 4 April 1954, and these improvements were introduced on the production line on the 144th aircraft, the earlier models being retrofitted.

A total of 535 Vampire trainers was ordered by the RAF, over a period of time, the initial unit deliveries being five aircraft to the CGS at Leconfield on 4 September 1952, followed by four delivered the same month to the APS at

Above left:
The Central Gunnery School at Leconfield used T11s for weapons training including firing of rocket projectiles and the standard four-cannon armament.

Left:
The Central Flying School at Little Rissington used T11s for the training of flying instructors. *Gloster*

Top:
Like a number of RAF fighter units, No 8 Squadron in Aden had a Vampire T11 for communications, continuation training and instrument rating.

Above:
T11s were used by No 3 CAACU at Exeter as high speed targets for the training of artillery gunners. The unit's pilots were the last regular operators of the aircraft in the UK. *Philip Birtles*

Acklington and No 202 AFS at Valley. Other early deliveries were to the APS at Sylt, No 233 OCU at Pembrey and No 229 OCU at Chivenor.

No 5 FTS at Oakington, near Cambridge, commenced the first Vampire advanced jet flying course in June 1954, the new students having graduated from the Percival Provost. The average to-solo time on the new aircraft was eight flying hours, the total course to wings standard involving 115 flying hours as well as ground instruction. The first course of students to receive all their advanced flying on jet aircraft were awarded their wings on 22 December 1954 at a parade at Oakington. The pilots were able to include fighter navigation training and experience compressibility effects before continuing on to weapons training.

In 1956 Vampire T11s replaced Balliol advanced trainers with the RAF College at Cranwell, and a number were also used by the CFS at Little Rissington to train instructors from 1959. The RAF became the first air force to conduct an all-through jet training programme, although grading training was later introduced to check initial pilot suitability. A number of Vampire T11s were allocated to fighter squadrons and some station flights for communications flying and to maintain a check on proficiency with instrument ratings and continuation training.

While the CFS was responsible for maintaining the high levels of flying instruction training, with regular checks at the various Flying Training Schools, the FWS at Leconfield was responsible for maintaining a high level of weapons training. A close liaison was maintained with operational units to keep up the high standard of pilot instructors with the squadron, as well as monitoring the weapons instructors at the Armament Practice

Schools. The staff at the FWS not only trained RAF aircrew, but also many overseas students.

With its good view and side-by-side seating the Vampire T11 was well suited to weapons training. Its pair of 20mm cannon could be used for air-to-air firing on towed targets, and rockets and practice bombs were carried for ground-attack training.

In addition to aircrew training, Vampire T11s were used on other training tasks. A number were allocated to the Central Navigation & Control School (CNCS) at Shawbury, together with Provosts, for the training of RAF air traffic controllers. This unit was the last in the RAF to operate the aircraft on training duties, the T11 providing realistic fast jet controlling exercises for the students until November 1970. No 3 CAACU at Exeter was equipped with a number of Vampire T11s in the early 1960s, replacing the veteran Mosquitos. The Vampires shared with Meteor T7s the duties of simulating tactical targets for Army gunners, to give them experience with high-speed, low-flying aircraft under typical battle conditions. The unit was disbanded in December 1971.

By 1965 No 1 FTS at Linton-on-Ouse was the only RAF unit still using the Vampire T11 for aircrew training, mostly for overseas students, alongside the unit's Jet Provosts. The small batch of T11s, supported by reserve aircraft held in store at No 27 MU, Shawbury, were transferred to No 7 FTS at Church Fenton in January 1966, followed by a move to No 3 FTS at Leeming on 1 November. They remained at Leeming for just over a year, and their withdrawal from service was marked by a small ceremony on a cold bright 29 November 1967.

The last RAF T11, XK637, flew from Chester on 8 November 1956, and was delivered to No 19 MU at St Athan on 27 November, along with XK636. XK637 served with No 4 FTS, RAF College at Cranwell and No 7 FTS before storage at Chester and Woodford. It was one of about 40 given away by Hawker Siddeley Aviation to schools, ATC cadet units and museums, this particular aircraft being acquired by No 1885 Squadron, ATC.

One Vampire T11 remains airworthy with the RAF. XH304 shares the limelight with a Meteor T7 as part of the Vintage Pair, administered by the

Above left:
WZ419 was the development T11 fitted with a pair of ejector seats under a clear view canopy, and dorsal fairings on the fins. Later production aircraft were built to this specification: earlier ones were modified.

Left:
The last RAF training unit equipped with Vampire T11s was No 3 FTS which used the aircraft for the instruction of foreign students. The aircraft were retired on 29 November 1967. *Philip Birtles*

49

Above left:
A total of 73 Vampire T Mk 22s was ordered by the RN, initially appearing to the early standard, but later modified. The first pre-production aircraft, WW458, made its maiden flight on 1 December 1951.

Left:
A small number of T22s were used by the FAA as admirals' barges and painted in a non-standard livery. *FAA Museum*

Top:
One of the FAA training units to use T22s was 738 Squadron, based at RNAS Lossiemouth. *FAA Museum*

Above:
Vampire T22 XA129 was used by Airwork at Yeovilton with the Air Directors School and is now preserved by the FAA Museum. *Philip Birtles*

A&AEE in August 1953 and XA102 was flown by the Handling Squadron for the compilation of pilots' notes. The first delivered were 11 aircraft, XA103 to XA113, to RNAS Stretton on 18 September 1953. The aircraft differed little from the RAF T11s except for their Naval equipment. They did not have arrester hooks, and initially ejector seats were not fitted, but a retrofit programme commenced in 1956 to correct this latter omission.

Vampire T22s entered FAA service with 740 Squadron at Lossiemouth, and were also used by 759 and 763 Squadrons at Lossiemouth, 738 Squadron at Brawdy, Airwork at Yeovilton and some of the FAA station flights. At least one was used as an Admiral's Barge, painted in a rather attractive navy blue livery. Production was completed with XG777, which was delivered to Lossiemouth on 25 May 1955, later serving with 738 Squadron. Following withdrawal from service in the mid-1960s, this aircraft was stored with others at No 5 MU Kemble before purchase by Hawker Siddeley Aviation, and became part of a batch dismantled and shipped to Chile at the end of 1972.

CFS which is now based at Scampton. At least one is also flown privately from time to time.

A total of 73 Vampire T22s was ordered for the Fleet Air Arm, all built at Christchurch. The first aircraft, XA100, flew in May 1953 and was allocated to company trials before delivery to Lossiemouth in July 1956. XA101 was flown to the

7
Vampire Trainers Overseas

With the excellent overseas market established by
de Havilland with the fighter and fighter-bombers,
many satisfied customers also showed interest in
the trainer. This not only provided them with a
cost effective multi-role advanced trainer, but also
took advantage of the commonality in spares and
support already firmly established.

The Australian Government became the first of
these customers when in 1951 it ordered 36
Vampire T33s for the RAAF, followed by five
T34s for the RAN. These aircraft were built
initially to the early RAF standard with the old
canopies and fins. However, by the time the order
was being completed, the new canopies were fitted
over ejector seats for the two crew, and the dorsal
fairings replaced the bullet shape on the fins. In
this up-to-date form the RAAF aircraft were

Below:
**New Zealand ordered six Vampire trainers as new
aircraft, and later acquired five ex-RAF T11s for
advanced training.** *RNZAF*

Above right:
**The SAAF T55s were equipped for full weapons
training, remaining in service until the 1970s.** *SAAF*

Centre right:
**The Vampire T55 was known as the J.28C in Sweden
and a number served with F5 training school.
Although the fins had been modified, the original
canopy was retained.** *RSAF*

Bottom right:
**The Vampire trainer continues in service for advanced
training with the Swiss Air Force. Comparison of this
photograph with that of the FB6 in chapter 4 gives a
good indication of the differences in configuration of
the two types.** *Philip Birtles*

The largest overseas order for Vampire trainers came from India with 53 being delivered from the UK and a further 60 built under licence. The early canopies were later replaced.

Lebanese Air Force T55 L151 was the first of four aircraft ordered, all of which were later fitted with the new canopy. Note the drop tanks fitted for the ferry flight.

The Iraqi Air Force ordered T55s for conversion training without ejector seats, the first aircraft, No 333, being delivered on 24 May 1953.

J-01 was the first of five T55s for Chile, an order to which was later added the demonstrator.

re-designated T35s, and were used for advanced flying and weapons training. The earlier aircraft were modified retrospectively as T.33As and T.34As, a further order being placed in 1955 for 68 T.35s and one T.34A to be produced under licence by de Havilland Australia. In addition four Vampire T.22s, including XG766 and XG770, were re-allocated from the FAA order and in mid-1954 equipped 724 Squadron RAN as its first jet aircraft.

New Zealand joined its neighbour by ordering six Vampire T55s, the export version, in late 1951. All six, NZ5701 to NZ5706, were for the RNZAF, and were built to the earlier configuration. The first was delivered on 27 April 1952, and five ex-RAF T11s fitted with ejector seats were later added. They served with No 75 Squadron until 1954, passing to the fighter Operational Conversion Unit formed at Okakea to take over jet aircrew training. The FOCU was disbanded at the end of June 1955, to be re-formed as the Jet Conversion Unit to operate the Vampires in the advanced training role. In early 1960 the JCU was replaced by the Bomber Conversion Unit which was equipped with Canberras, two Vampire FB5s and four Vampire trainers for bomber aircrew conversion. No 75 Squadron re-equipped on 1 September 1963 with eight FB5s and four trainers until Skyhawks were delivered in May

1970. The Vampires passed to No 14 Squadron, where they remained until retirement at the end of 1972, to be replaced by Strikemasters.

The next customer was the South African Air Force, which ordered an initial batch of six Vampire T55s powered by Goblin 35 engines to the early RAF standard and fitted with four 20mm cannon under the fuselage. Provision was made under the wings for the carriage of bombs, rockets and a pair of 100gal drop tanks. The first of these aircraft, SA221, was delivered on 26 May 1952 for operational conversion training to the single-seat Vampires and later Sabres. A further order followed for 19 Vampire T55s, commencing SA257, to the later standard with ejector seats,

Right:
Finland ordered nine Vampire T55s for conversion and advanced training: here VT-1 and VT-2, without ejector seats, are ready for delivery from Hatfield.

Below:
The Union of Burma was a new Vampire customer when it ordered eight trainers as its first jet aircraft.

Facing page:
The Egyptian Air Force used a dozen Vampire trainers to prepare pilots for flying the Soviet MiG-15s.

and the earlier aircraft were modified. One of these aircraft was still flying in the late 1970s for displays at air shows.

The first European order came for six Vampire T55s for the Royal Norwegian Air Force, to the same basic standard as the SAAF aircraft. The first, PX-E, was delivered on 28 July 1952 to No 337 Squadron at Gardermoen, but in 1955 they all returned to Britain to be overhauled by Marshalls as XJ771 to XJ776, for the RAF.

Venezuela ordered one T55, 23-A-36, which was delivered on 16 September 1952 to the same standard and armament as the SAAF aircraft. Five more were ordered on 17 April 1958, the first (2E-35) being delivered on 30 May for jet conversion training with the *Escuadrón de Caza No 35* at the Mariscal Sucre airbase.

Below:
The eight T55s for Indonesia were not fitted with ejector seats. They were used for advanced training and ground attack duties, and had four cannon and rocket rails.

Bottom:
One Vampire T55, 63-5571, was delivered to Japan in 1955 for evaluation, but no further orders resulted. The aircraft is preserved at Gifu Air Base.

A new customer was the Portuguese Army Air Force, which ordered two T55s to the early standard with provision for the fitment of cannon and bomb and rocket carriers. These aircraft (P.5801 and P.5802) were delivered on 4 December 1952 to Ota airbase near Lisbon.

The Royal Swedish Air Force became one of the largest Vampire trainer customers when it ordered 45 Goblin 3-powered aircraft, the first 30 to the earlier modification standard with provision for the fitment of cannon, bomb and rocket carriers, and Swedish drop tanks. The first batch, 28411 to 28440, was delivered between 16 February and 10 November 1953 allowing the first advanced pilot training course to commence at F5 Wing, Ljunbyhed in Southern Sweden in March 1954. The students completed 75 hours initial training on Safirs, followed by 100 hours advanced training on Vampires, before converting to the jet fighters. The remaining 15 aircraft, 28441 to 28455, were delivered at the end of 1955 and had ejector seats, the new canopy and dorsal fairings.

The Swiss Air Force had a need for an advanced jet trainer to convert its pilots to Vampires and other jet combat aircraft. Initially three Vampire T11s, U-1001 to U-1003, were supplied in 1953 for

evaluation, fitted with the dorsal fin fairings, but still had the early canopies without ejector seats. The next order, following successful evaluation, came in 1956, for a further seven aircraft to the improved T55 standard with the clear view canopy and ejector seats for the two crew, and in 1960 the three initial aircraft, which by now had become U-1201 to U-1203, were brought up to the same standard. The training load increased from the straight-forward conversion task, to include a full programme of advanced blind flying training as a follow-on to the basic training in the Pilatus P3. As a result, a further 20 Vampire T55s were ordered in 1958, all the aircraft being equipped for armament training with four cannon and under-wing bomb and rocket launchers. For these aircraft de Havilland supplied the wooden fuselage nacelle and Goblin 3 engines, while F&W at Emmen built all the metal parts under licence. However, there were still insufficient Vampire trainers, so nine ex-RAF aircraft were purchased from de Havilland in 1967 and transported by road to Altensheim in Switzerland, where they were completely overhauled by the Flug & Fahrzeung-werke (FFA) as U-1231 to U-1239. Two aircraft in the 1958 order, U-1211 and U-1219, were fitted with remote controlled nose mounted cine cameras. The Vampire trainer continues to serve in small numbers with the Swiss Air Force, and retirement does not appear to be imminent.

The largest overseas order for Vampire trainers came from India for 53 T55s powered by the Goblin 35 engine and built to the latter standard with ejector seats. Four cannon were fitted, with provision for the carriage of bombs, rockets and drop tanks. The first, IY467, was delivered on 12 May 1953 and the last, BY-386, on 6 February 1958. Meanwhile a further 60 were built under licence by the Hindustan Aeronautics at Bangalore.

The Lebanon ordered one Vampire T55 with ejector seats, four cannons and the usual provision for underwing stores, L151 being delivered on 24 August 1953 to Kleyate for jet conversion duties. Three more aircraft were soon added to complement L151.

The Iraqi Air Force required a trainer to convert its pilots on to its Vampires, and ordered seven T55s without ejector seats but with the full armament provision: the first, '333', was delivered on 24 May 1953.

In 1956 demonstrator Vampire T55 G-AOXH was shipped from Chester to Buenos Aires, and assembled at the Argentine Air Force Base at Moron. Flown by George Errington on 15 December, it commenced a 30,000-mile tour of Argentina, Peru, Uruguay and Chile arriving in Chile on 16 April 1957. It was handed over to the Chilean

Air Force to add to the five T01s and T05s ordered on 22 October 1953, the first of which was delivered on 10 June 1954. By 1972 only one remained serviceable. To overcome the shortage of suitable trainers, six ex-RN Vampire T22s were removed from store at St Athan, packed at Chester and shipped to Chile, where they were overhauled for service.

On 23 March 1955 the Finnish Air Force ordered four T55s, later increased to nine, powered by Goblin 35 engines but without ejector seats. Only two cannon were fitted and the usual underwing stores could be carried. The aircraft were used for flying conversion to the Vampire FB52s and later for advanced training in prep-aration for the Folland Gnat.

A new Vampire customer was the Union of Burma Air Force, which ordered eight T55s in 1954 to the later standard, as part of its modernisation programme. Only two cannon were fitted in addition to the underwing stores capability, and the first four aircraft, UB.501 to UB.504, were delivered to Mingaladon Air Base near Rangoon on 7 December 1954.

To add to its Vampire FB9s, the Southern Rhodesia Air Force acquired eight ex-RAF Vampire T11s. These were delivered from Benson to Salisbury in the spring of 1956, the 5,500nm ferry flight being accomplished in seven stages. Four more ex-RAF T11s were soon added, and the aircraft continued to operate with No 2 Squadron into the early 1970s.

In the spring of 1955 Egypt placed an order for 12 Vampire trainers without ejector seats, but with full armament capability. The first, No 1570, was delivered on 6 July the same year to Fayid to be used for advanced training to prepare student pilots for flying the Soviet supplied MiG-15s.

Another new Vampire customer was Indonesia, which ordered eight T.55s to the later standard, fitted with four cannon and stores carriers for bombs, rockets and fuel tanks. Indonesia was the 19th customer, and by this time over 800 Vampire trainers were in service world-wide. The eight aircraft, J.701 to J.708, were shipped on 29 December 1955, and after assembly they were handed over on 20 February 1956 at Hussean Air Base, Bandung to form the Indonesian Air Force's first jet squadron.

Vampire trainer No 63-5571, built to the latest standard and fitted with ejector seats, was delivered to Japan on 8 November 1955 for evaluation by the Air Self Defence Force. It was not adopted, but the aircraft was retained by the experimental squadron. It was later preserved at Gifu Air Base.

The Arab Legion Air Force, later to become the Royal Jordanian Air Force, acquired two ex-RAF

Vampire T11s without ejector seats in 1955. In 1960 a further ex-RAF aircraft to the later standard was added. The aircraft were used initially to convert pilots to fly the Vampire FB9s, and later as advanced trainers to prepare pilots for the more sophisticated Hunters.

From nearer at home came an order for three T55s for the Irish Air Corps in early 1956. They were to the later standard with ejector seats, but armament was limited to two cannon and rocket carriers only. The first aircraft, No 185, was delivered on 15 May 1956, followed by Nos 186 and 187 on 20 July, for jet conversion training and fighter/ground-attack duties. Three more T55s, Nos 191-193, were added in early 1961, and an ex-RAF T11 was delivered on 30 August 1963 for ground instruction of maintenance engineers.

Two frustrated overseas orders were from Ceylon and Syria. The Ceylon Government ordered five T55s in 1951; these were packed and shipped to Colombo. After unloading at the docks, however, the decision was changed, and they were returned to Britain unpacked. No records exist of their ultimate fate, although they were probably used for spares. The Syrian order was for two T55s to the latest standard with full armament and stores provision, placed in early 1956. They were ready for delivery in July 1956, but an embargo was placed by the British Government on arms supply to Syria and both aircraft were stored at Hatfield until scrapped in the early 1960s.

In January 1957 the Austrian Air Force became the final Vampire trainer customer when it ordered three T55s to the latest standard with ejector seats and full provision for armament and stores carriage. The first, 5C-YA, was delivered on 26 March, only two months after the order, and two more were ordered in January 1961. Austria had a further requirement after the production line had closed down, acquiring three ex-RAF T11s in January 1964. The aircraft operated first from Graz/Thalerhof and later Hörsching near Linz, and returned regularly to Chester for overhaul, where one of the aircraft crashed on a test flight. This aircraft was replaced by an ex-RAF T11 and the last was retired in 1971.

Below:
One of the frustrated export orders was for Vampire T55s Nos 493 and 494 for Syria, which were embargoed by the British Government.

Bottom:
The Austrian Air Force was the ultimate customer for the T55, later aircraft coming from RAF stocks. The original 5C-YA crashed in Snowdonia while on a test flight after returning to the UK for overhaul; the 5C-YA shown here is an ex-RAF replacement.
Philip Birtles

8
The Venom Fighter-Bombers

The Venom, originally known as the Vampire FB8, was designed to specification F.15/49 as an interim replacement for the Vampire fighter-bombers, pending the late introduction of Hunters and Swifts to the RAF. In fact the Supermarine Swift proved almost totally unsatisfactory, and the Hawker Hunter did not make a suitable ground-attack aircraft until the FGA9 entered service. Therefore, Venoms served more widely and remained in operation much longer than antici-pated, the final ones being retired from active duties in Switzerland in August 1983.

Although the Venom had the same basic layout as the Vampire, it differed in a number of significant aspects. Power came from a 4,850lb thrust Ghost 103 engine, and to take advantage of this a new wing was designed with a leading edge

sweepback of 17° 6', and the thickness/chord ratio reduced from 14% to 10%. The wing trailing edge was straight and the structure was stressed for the installation of a pair of 75gal wing tip tanks in addition to the underwing stores positions, allowing full combat manoeuvring while full. The wing tip tanks were not jettisonable in flight, but were an optional fit if required.

Below:
The prototype Venom FB1, VV612, first flew on 1 September 1949 and appeared at the SBAC display at Farnborough a few days later.

Bottom:
The second prototype Venom FB1, VV613, was used to test the carriage of a pair of wing tip tanks and underwing drop tanks.

The De Havilland Venom F Mk1 (DH112).
James Goulding

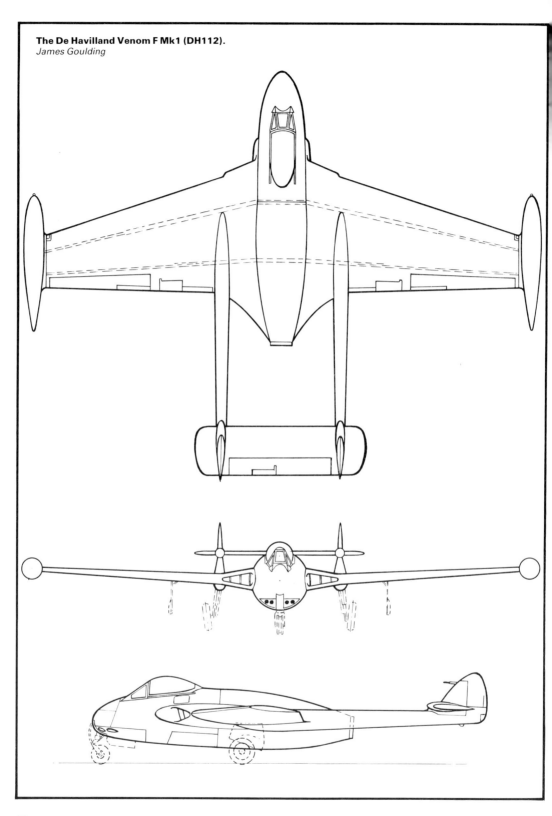

The prototype Venom FB1, VV612, made its first flight from Hatfield piloted by John Derry on 2 September 1949 and, following company flight trials, was delivered to the A&AEE Boscombe Down for testing in May 1950. The aircraft was considered reasonably satisfactory, but further refinement was required. Despite some faults which needed correction, the aircraft showed a noticeable advantage in mock combat with two current fighters, a creditable performance in view of the fact that the Venom was optimised for ground attack.

The second prototype, VV613, joined the development programme on 23 July 1950 and was delivered to the A&AEE on 3 April 1951 for further trials to assess any improvements. It was found that the rate of roll without wing tip tanks was poor, but with them fitted it was deplorable. The wings had drooped leading edges in an effort to cure a nose pitch-up at medium and high altitudes, but the first production aircraft, WE255, had this problem return with the deterioration of the wing surface. However, the aircraft had been

Below:
The first production Venom FB1, WE255, carried out underwing bomb carrying trials.

Bottom:
The early Venom FB1s which performed operational trials with No 11 Squadron had red bands painted on the wings to signify that only restricted manoeuvres were allowed. *Flight*

flown at altitudes up to 51,000ft with reasonably satisfactory control characteristics.

Regret was expressed at Boscombe Down at the lack of ejector seat for the pilot, but it was to be fitted in later production aircraft. Other external changes from the Vampire included wing fences to eliminate tip stall on the approach to landing, and bullet fairings at the fin and tailplane junction, although the later Venom FB4 had flatter-topped rudders with a trailing edge bullet fairing added. Fixed armament of the Venom was four under-nose mounted 20mm Hispano Mk V cannon. Two 1,000lb bombs or eight 60lb rockets could be carried on underwing pylons.

Meanwhile the first prototype was delivered to the de Havilland Engine Co at Hatfield on 18 December 1950 to have a two-position reheat fitted to the Ghost engine. The second prototype ended its days on ground instruction duties at RNAS Arbroath as A.2327 in 1955.

The first six production Venoms, WE255 to WE260, were flown by the A&AEE and the manufacturer on trials. WE255 was used for aerodynamic and controllability development including the measurement of control column forces. It eventually became 7187M at No 2 School of Technical Training on 7 February 1955. WE256

was used for a variety of trial installations and fuel tests, before undertaking gun firing trials at Boscombe Down. It was retired to No 19MU at St Athan as 7228M on 7 July 1955. WE257 was the high speed development aircraft delivered to Boscombe Down on 9 January 1952. It went to the Handling Squadron at Manby on 16 April for the compilation of pilot's notes and was retired to ground training at Halton as 7133M on 18 March 1954. WE258 was delivered to Boscombe Down on 12 February 1952, WE259 first flew on 28 November 1951, going to Boscombe the following 9 January, and WE260 first flew on 29 December 1951 for stick shaker and power control development, passing to the A&AEE on 25 April.

The first delivery to the RAF was of WE263 to the Central Fighter Establishment (CFE) at West Raynham on 21 April 1952. It was joined by WE265 on 25 April and WE261 on 8 May for full service evaluation before entry into squadron service.

WE262 was used for the evaluation of a redesigned instrument panel and tip tank trials in 1952, ending up as 7134M at Halton on 18 March 1954. WE265 first flew on 2 May 1952 and was delivered to Christchurch for development flying on 15 May. It was joined by WE269 on 4 July, but WE265 left for Boscombe on 27 August.

WE266 first flew on 3 April 1952 and was retained by de Havilland for development flying, going to Nameo in Canada in late 1952 for cold weather trials. It retired to Halton as 7211M on 24 May 1955. WE267 was delivered to the RAE Farnborough on 8 May 1952, later to be joined by WE268.

Above:
No 94 Squadron, which formed an aerobatic team, was part of the Venom-equipped No 121 Wing at Fassberg.

After the first 15 production aircraft were built at Hatfield, the production line was moved to the larger Chester factory, the first aircraft (WE270) being delivered to No 22 MU on 26 July 1952. Small batches were also assembled by Fairey Aviation at Ringway and Marshalls of Cambridge. Plans were also made for the Bristol Aeroplane Co at Filton, to build a further 132 FB1s commencing WL892, but these were cancelled before completion of any of the aircraft. A total of 375 Venom FB1s were built for the RAF, mainly at Chester, the last one, WR273, being delivered to No 29 MU on 29 December 1954.

Venoms continued in a variety of trials and development work, WE272 being used for flutter checks after delivery to Boscombe on 1 September 1952. WE275 was a Hatfield assembled aircraft, out of sequence, which was delivered to Christchurch on 30 June 1952 for high altitude development flying. WE279 was delivered to Folland on 4 September 1952 for trials work, and WE280 was delivered to A&AEE on 27 January 1953. Following its demonstration at the SBAC display at Farnborough in September 1952, WE281 was used for high Mach number flutter trials in 1953. WE315 was delivered to Christchurch on 1 February 1953 as the first aircraft fitted with ejector seat. The CFE also operated WE313 and WE314, both being delivered on 9 March 1953.

No single-seat Venoms operated with RAF squadrons in Britain, but they served widely in the 2nd Tactical Air Force in Germany, and in the high temperatures of Cyprus, the Middle East, Africa and Asia.

The first overseas unit to receive Venoms was No 11 Squadron at Wunstorf in Germany, which exchanged its Vampires in August 1952 and was responsible for the operational service trials. These early aircraft suffered from weaknesses in the wing structure, which subjected them to flight limitations; as a warning, broad orange bands were painted across the wings. The aircraft were first operated on a trial basis in the NATO Exercise 'Mainbrace', a largely Naval exercise. Four Venoms from No 11 Squadron were joined by two more from the CFE for Exercise 'Hold Fast' from 15 to 23 September.

During the early days with the Venoms No 11 Squadron found that some of the other NATO air forces were unfamiliar with cartridge starting procedures. It only needed the sight of a line-up of Venoms belching flame and black smoke out of the top of the engine cowlings to cause the alarm to be sounded. By the time the emergency services had arrived, the aircraft would be taxying for take-off, unaware of the problems caused.

The earlier aircraft with No 11 Squadron were replaced with more combat-ready examples while Nos 266 (Rhodesia) and 5 Squadrons re-equipped with Venoms at Wunstorf, forming No 123 Wing in February 1954. By this time the first aircraft with ejector seats fitted had been issued. Squadron pilots were well satisfied with the performance of the Venom: it proved to be an outstanding

Top:
The Venoms of No 11 Squadron used the Fassberg range for air-to-ground firings. *Air Ministry*

Above:
Based at Tengah in Singapore, the RNZAF No 14 Squadron hired its Venom FB1s from the RAF.

Left:
No 6 Squadron re-equipped with FB1s at Amman in February 1954. *RAF*

interceptor and ground attack aircraft, fitting in well between the heavy load carrying Thunderjet and the transonic Sabre. The Venom was also able to account well for itself in combat with swept wing aircraft, especially above 35,000ft, its rate of climb being a great advance over the Vampire.

The second Venom wing, No 121, was formed at Fassberg in mid-1953, and consisted of Nos 14, 98 and 118 Squadrons; the third and final Venom wing in 2TAF was No 139 at Celle, formed during the early part of 1954 and comprising Nos 16, 94 and 145 Squadrons. All had converted from Vampires. The Fassberg wing changed its Venoms for Hunters in 1955 and the Celle wing disbanded in 1957.

Above:
The Venoms of No 5 Squadron have used a cartridge start with its familiar plume of smoke. No 5 Squadron was one of the Wunstorf based units. *Flight*

To achieve early familiarisation, No 14 Squadron was issued with some of the stress-limited aircraft from No 11 Squadron, but they were replaced within two months of the Squadron re-equipping in May 1953.

Despite the overall success of the introduction of the Venoms, the aircraft were not totally without problems, and No 14 Squadron had its share to deal with. The Squadron was tasked with series of bombing trials, including dive-bombing from medium and low levels. On 23 March, during the pull-out of one of the medium-level trials, the starboard wing of WE368 came off. As the remainder of the aircraft began to break up, the pilot, Flg Off D'Arcy, pulled the ejector seat handle and made the first RAF ejection through the canopy. In the resulting investigation the weakness was found to be in the rear spar and checks revealed that 75% of the remaining Venoms suffered the same defect. An immediate modification programme was initiated to overcome the problem.

Another problem was a series of mysterious crashes, where the evidence had been destroyed by fire. However, in November 1954 Fl Lt Severne of No 98 Squadron experienced a fire warning, following which he was able to make a successful forced landing on the Fassberg crash strip. He jumped out of his aircraft quickly, and by hacking off the engine cowlings with an axe, he was able to direct a carbon dioxide extinguisher on to the fire, saving the evidence. The accident investigation found that, under certain conditions of zero 'g', fuel was venting from the fuselage into the engine cooling air scoops, resulting in flash fires. For his action Fl Lt Severne was awarded the Air Force Cross.

With these early problems overcome, the Venom was found to be ideal for ground attack, due to its manoeuvrability, steadiness as a gun platform, its good endurance, ease of handling and the ability to carry a wide range of stores. Typical practice missions were fighter-bomber attacks on small ground targets such as bridges and road convoys; Army close support; airfield defence against air attack; and visual reconnaissance. The Venoms had an advantage in air-to-air combat, as by using their greater manoeuvrability, they could fly rings round many modern fighters. The major shortcoming was a lack of high top speed for the interception of any fast hostile aircraft. From the point of view of servicing and engineering support, the aircraft was operated within the Wing, but each squadron retained its identity with the commanding officer being responsible for training, discipline and morale.

In April 1954 details were released of the improved Venom FB4. It was an all-round improvement in detailed design, but the most noticeable change was the revision of the shape of the rudder to prevent excessive yaw and possible rudder locking at low speeds. The FB4 was fitted with hydraulically operated ailerons to give improved control at high Mach numbers, and could carry underwing fuel tanks, in addition to the tip tanks. Design work on this version had been transferred to Christchurch and FB1 WE381 was taken from the Chester production line for conversion at Christchurch as the prototype FB4. After modification WE381 was delivered to Boscombe Down on 18 May 1954, where the dropping of the underwing fuel tanks was included in its testing. It finished its flying at Farnborough where it was scrapped in 1950.

A total of 151 Venom FB4s was built for the RAF, 52 from Chester, 51 from Hatfield, 33 from Marshalls and 15 from Fairey. None appears to have been used for development flying, the majority being issued to the squadrons. The first production aircraft, WR374, was delivered to No 29 MU at High Ercall on 28 March 1955, and the ulimate single-seat Venom for the RAF was WR564, delivered to No 22 MU on 28 March 1956, later serving with No 28 Squadron.

The only unit in 2TAF to re-equip with FB4s was No 123 Wing at Wunstorf, starting with No 5 Squadron in July 1955. No 11 Squadron received its aircraft in August and No 266 (Rhodesia) Squadron in May 1956. No 121 Wing at Fassberg left its aircraft and went by road to Jever to collect its Hunters, and No 139 Squadron operated a few FB4s until disbandment of the squadrons, No 16 September 1957, No 94 on the 15th of the same month, and No 145 one month later on 15 October.

At this time No 123 Wing began the withdrawal of the Venoms, with No 5 Squadron the first to go on 12 October, followed by Nos 11 and 266 Squadrons by the end of November. Also in Germany No 213 Squadron re-formed as a Canberra attack unit on 1 September 1955, and worked up with Venoms until Canberra B(I)6s were delivered in March 1956.

As already mentioned the Venoms served widely overseas, in addition to West Germany. No 6 Squadron was the first Middle Eastern unit to fly them when FB1s were delivered to Amman in Jordan in February 1954. A move was made in June to Habbaniya in Iraq where the unit joined No 73 Squadron, whose pilots replaced their Vampires with Venoms in December. No 249 Squadron began to re-equip with Venoms at Amman in October 1954, remaining there until 1956, when it moved to Akrotiri in Cyprus.

On 15 September 1954 No 32 Squadron in Egypt moved from Deversoir with its Vampires, to Kabrit, on the south side of the Great Bitter Lake. To the pilots' surprise a pair of Venom FB1s were awaiting them and by the following January the Squadron was fully re-equipped. Despite a struggle to keep the aircraft serviceable because of a lack of spares, a move was made to Shaibah, via Amman, on 14 January, where the unit remained until moving to Takali in Malta in October 1955.

No 8 Squadron was the only other Middle Eastern Venom unit, exchanging its Vampire FB9s at Khormaksar, Aden in June 1955. The Squadron had received its standard at Khormaksar on 9 April 1954 and at that time had served in Aden and the surrounding area for over 27 years, making it the senior fighting unit in the Protectorate. The Squadron used its aircraft actively against rebel tribesmen as a protection for the local sheikhs and

their oil installations. Detachments were frequently made to Shajah, where the ground crews had to maintain the aircraft in temperatures of 65°C without shade, making the aircraft too hot to touch. During these detachments spares were often a problem, and when an engine access panel was damaged, the only way to make a repair was to manufacture a patch from bright yellow beer cans.

On 23 December 1954, not long after re-equipping with Venoms, No 73 Squadron had four of its aircraft airborne when a sandstorm hit the airfield at Habbaniya. The pilots were forced to abandon their aircraft, which they achieved successfully, and by February 1955 when they visited Nicosia in Cyprus, replacement aircraft had been supplied. Following a month of exercises the Squadron flew the 580 miles to its base in 1 hour and 5 minutes.

On 2 May 1955 the RAF handed over Habbaniya to the Royal Iraqi Air Force and No 73 Squadron withdrew to Nicosia. No 6 Squadron remained until April 1956 when it moved to Akrotiri, having become the first unit to receive FB4s in July 1955. In August four of the new aircraft completed a 10,000-mile flight from Habbaniya to Cape Town and back, during which they broke the record from Cape Town to Pretoria, previously held by the SAAF. They covered the 807 miles in 1 hour 23 minutes, nine minutes faster than the previous record. Operation 'Quick Return' (as the mass flight was called) resulted in the first visit of RAF Venoms as far south as Cape Town; under the command of Flt Lt Michael Hobson the four aircraft completed the round trip in 14 days, during which they visited 13 airfields giving displays of formation aerobatics. Engineering support was provided by a Valetta of No 114 Squadron.

Most of the Venom squadrons in the region joined other British and French forces in active duty during the seven-day Suez crisis from 1 November 1956. The Akrotiri-based No 6 Squadron made the first Venom strike against Egypt led by its Commanding Officer, Sqn Ldr P. C. Ellis DFC, when rockets were fired at ground targets. During the campaign one Venom was lost.

Some of the Middle East-based squadrons re-equipped with the improved FB4s in 1956, including Nos 8, 249 and 73 Squadrons, which received its first aircraft on 19 December. There was not time for No 23 Squadron to re-equip as it was moved from its post-Suez crisis base at Mafraq to Nicosia in January 1957. There its 13 Venom FB1s, two Vampire T11s and a Meteor T7 were replaced by Canberra B2s, the last Venoms departing on 14 January.

During 1957 the Venoms of Nos 8 and 249 Squadrons were contributing towards the control of the Aden-Yemen borders, as well as operating against rebel tribesmen in Trucial Oman. In

No 8 Squadron operated its FB4s in the hot, barren climate of Aden.

reports from Aden of hostilities on the Protectorate's frontier with Yemen, the Venoms were in action against Yemeni troops in at least three areas, including Beihan, where incursions had been made. The Venoms supported troops of the Durham Light Infantry, attacking with rockets and cannon fire. No 73 Squadron also took part in these activities, firing live rockets and cannon for the first time on 30 August 1956 on ground targets at Al Talela. The Squadron had however, moved to Akrotiri by the end of March 1957, and converted to Canberras.

No 6 Squadron had moved to Akrotiri in April 1956 and by July 1957 had converted to Canberras, followed by No 249 Squadron the next month. This only left No 8 Squadron in Aden flying Venoms until re-equipping with Hunter FGA9s by 7 March 1960.

In Asia No 60 Squadron, which had been the first Far East Air Force jet squadron, exchanged its Vampires for Venom FB1s on 24 April 1955, at Tengah, Singapore. At this time No 14 (NZ) Squadron moved from Cyprus to Tengah where RAF Venom FB1s were awaiting, on hire to the New Zealand Government, consolidating the Australian and New Zealand forces. Nos 60 and 14 (NZ) Squadrons flew together in the Malayan Emergency, making ground attack stikes on terrorist positions often close to allied troops, operations requiring a high level of accuracy.

Further north at Butterworth in Malaya, No 45 Squadron received the first of 18 aircraft, FB1 WR346, on 10 October 1955, and had completed

equipping by the following February. It also took an active part in the Malayan Emergency, making some 300 strikes against terrorist locations before the Venoms were retired by 15 November 1957.

No 14 (NZ) Squadron left Tengah for New Zealand on 30 June 1958 to re-equip with Canberras, leaving behind its Venoms. During their stay at Singapore, the squadron pilots had formed an aerobatic team, one of the specialities being the writing of the figure '14' in smoke.

The FB1s of No 60 Squadron were replaced by FB4s in April 1957 and they continued in operation in Singapore until replaced by Meteor NF14s in October 1959. The last of its Venoms joined No 28 Squadron in Hong Kong on 13 November 1959.

Based at Sek Kong, six miles from the communist border, No 28 Squadron had received its first FB1, WR299 'A', in February 1956, and its duties included patrolling the 'bamboo curtain'. The airfield was one of the most demanding in the RAF, with its single runway surrounded on three sides by high mountains. Take-offs were made towards the gap, and landings in the opposite direction, made even more hazardous by the regular strong cross-winds. In June 1957 the airfield was relegated to emergency use only, and No 28 Squadron moved to the main airport of Hong Kong, Kai Tak. Re-equipment with FB4s

69

was completed there, the normal duties of the Squadron being daily armed reconnaissance flights by the duty pair of aircraft, the object being to spot pirate junks and any illegal activity in the Pearle Estuary. During the summer months, patrolling off the more popular beaches was added to the tasks, to warn of sharks and manta rays. When two of the Venoms collided at 30,000ft about 40 miles out to sea, both pilots ejected successfully and parachuted into the water. They were picked up fairly quickly by a Chinese fishing boat, whose crew received as a reward, a scroll recording the rescue, an enormous sack of rice and $1,000. No 28 Squadron became the last RAF unit to operate Venoms, until WR539 'F' flew the last sortie on 27 June 1962, Hunter FGA9s being the replacement aircraft.

Although No 28 Squadron was the last unit to operate Venoms, it was not the last unit to be re-equipped with the aircraft. No 142 Squadron was re-formed at Eastleigh, Nairobi on 1 February 1959 with Venom FB4s, led by Sq Ldr Ramirez. Soon after, on 30 March, it was renumbered No 208 Squadron, which had previously been operating Hunter F6s at Akrotiri. The new No 208 Squadron was soon involved in training, going on detachment to the Royal Rhodesian Air Force base at Thornhill for armament practice. A tour of Rhodesia and Nyasaland followed, before

returning to Kenya. During the following months the Squadron participated in various exercises and formed an aerobatic team, which in August performed before the Sultan of Zanzibar to celebrate his 80th birthday. No 208 Squadron continued to fly effectively in Africa and the Persian Gulf, operations ranging from the Northern Frontier District of Kenya on Army co-operation exercises with 24 Brigade, to Khormaksar, Sharjah and Bahrain. Many of the Venoms began to show their age and were scrapped as they became time-expired, the Squadron finally returning to Britain on 24 March 1960 to re-equip with Hunter FGA9s at Stradishall.

Below:
The Royal Iraqi Air Force operated two squadrons of Venoms, one of ex-RAF Mk 1s and the other of newly-built FB50s.

Bottom:
Venezuela ordered 22 Venom FB54s, the export version of the FB4. *Venezuela*

Above right:
The Swiss Air Force was a major user of the Venom, with FB1s, FB4s and a specially adapted reconnaissance version. They were finally retired at the end of 1983. *Philip Birtles*

Export Customers

Although the Venom was produced as a relatively short-life interim aircraft, it proved to be a successful export product, following in the footsteps of the Vampire. Its relatively uncomplicated development, together with large orders for the RAF, made the Venom a very cost-effective acquisition for a number of air forces. The export version of the Venom fighter-bomber was known as the FB50.

The first overseas customer was the Italian Air Force, which ordered two FB50s, MM6153 and MM6154, both delivered on 21 February 1953, to be followed by licence production by Fiat. In the event these plans did not materialise and no Venoms were built in Italy.

With the Royal Iraqi Air Force taking over responsibility for the defence of its country, a batch of FB1s were supplied to equip No 5 Squadron. The first one was delivered to Habbaniya in May 1954, by George Thornton, a de Havilland test pilot, in a time of 6 hours 25 minutes, and the Squadron was completely equipped by early 1955. An order followed for 15 FB50s, Nos 352 to 366, to equip No 6 Squadron, also at Habbaniya. They were delivered between 8 April 1955 and 3 February 1956.

In July 1955 Venezuela ordered 22 FB54s, the export version of the FB4, all of which were built at Chester. The first aircraft, 1A-34, was delivered to No 34 Squadron at Maiquetta on 1 December 1955, and the final one, 8C-34, on 17 August, 1956. They remained in service until the end of 1965 when they were replaced by Hawker Hunters.

The major overseas user of the Venom was the Swiss Air Force, which undertook a detailed evaluation in both Britain and Switzerland. After a successful conclusion, licence production commenced in 1953 of 126 FB1s (J-1501 to J-1625) at F&W Emmen, Doflug Altenshein and Pilatus AG Stans. It was also decided to build the Ghost 48 engine in Switzerland, licence production being the responsibility of Sulzer Brothers at Winter-

thur. However, because of a lack of engine manufacturing experience, compared with that for airframes, the first 35 engines were supplied direct by de Havilland, and Swiss-built Ghost engines were installed in the 30th and subsequent aircraft. The production rate eventually achieved six aircraft per month.

Because of delays in the selection of a new combat aircraft by the Swiss Government, the Venoms had to continue in operation much longer than anticipated. Although the wooden fuselage did not suffer from fatigue, the metal structure began to show signs of age. Extensive fatigue testing was carried out by F&W at Emmen, and as a result a number of strengthening modifications were made, more than doubling the service life of the aircraft. Monitoring of the structural condition continued during the life of the aircraft to avoid any restrictions being imposed on the normal operations.

In 1956 the same group of factories produced 24 reconnaissance versions of the Venom FB1, serials commencing at J-1626. In addition to the standard equipment, these Venoms, known as FB1Rs, had fixed underwing fuel tanks with a number of automatic aerial cameras installed in the forward portion. When the replacement Mirage IIIR reconnaissance aircraft were delivered in 1969, the special Venoms were reduced to eight aircraft retained for training purposes, the remainder being converted to the normal combat standard.

Finally, in 1956 100 Venom FB4s equipped with UHF radio and an improved bomb sight were licence-built, commencing J-1701.

The Swiss Air Force Venoms were used mainly in the ground attack role. In 1965 a total of 11 combat Staffeln were equipped with Venoms, crewed by the part-time militia pilots, and in the early 1970s, when some of the aircraft were 16 years old, some 200 were still in service with 14 squadrons. The final aircraft were withdrawn in the latter half of 1983, a number being sold to enthusiasts for preservation.

9
Venom Night Fighters

The two-seat Venom NF2 was developed by de Havilland from the single-seat Venom, in a similar way to the early Vampire night fighter from the Vampire fighter-bomber. The Venom Wings, tail and engine installation were retained, but a new fuselage nacelle was designed to accommodate a pilot and observer side-by-side, and the AI radar was located in the lengthened nose. The prototype, G-5-3, was produced as a private venture by de Havilland, and was flown by John Derry from Hatfield for the first time on 22 August 1950, powered by a 4,850lb thrust Ghost 103 engine. The first public appearance was at the SBAC display at Farnborough the following month.

The prototype was adopted by the RAF as WP227 when it was delivered to Boscombe Down on 3 April 1951 for evaluation until September. During preliminary handling trials the rate of roll was found to be barely adequate for a night fighter, and would be totally unsuitable for all-weather operations. Great regret was expressed at the lack of any intention to fit ejector seats for the crew, although the good all-round view and roominess of the cockpit was praised.

The first seven of the 90 production Venom NF2s were built at Hatfield, commencing with WL804 which first flew on 4 March 1952 but was destroyed in a crash early in its development

programme. WL805 and WL807 were used for control development at Christchurch and WL806 was delivered to Boscombe Down on 11 September 1952. WL808 flew on elevator dither and buffet trials, before going to Boscombe Down on 25 February 1953 and later to CFE at West Raynham. WL809 and WL812 were evaluated by NATO, WL809 then going to Boscombe on 5 January 1953 and WL812 to de Havilland Propellers on 8 January. WL810 had dorsal fin fairings and flew on underwing drop fuel tank trials at Christchurch. The new clear view canopy was tried on WL811 at Christchurch, the first NF2 off the Chester production line. WL814 was used to check the new large chord elevator and dorsal fin installation before going to the A&AEE. WL813 was delivered to de Havilland Propellers on 5 December 1952, followed by WL820 on 9 June 1953, both aircraft being allocated to Firestreak air-to-air missile development.

The first delivery to the RAF was WL817 to the Handling Squadron at Manby on 6 May 1953 for the compilation of pilots' notes, and WL816 and WL818 were delivered to the CFE at West Raynham on 22 May. The first squadron aircraft were delivered from the production line in one side of Hawarden airfield to No 48 MU on the other side.

The first squadron to equip with Venom NF2s was at Coltishall in December 1953. The Squadron made its operational debut in Exercise 'Dividend' in July 1954, but because of a high accident rate when pilots found themselves in difficulties at night on the approach, it was the only unit to operate the basic NF2s.

In an effort to overcome these difficulties, the surviving NF2s were fitted with jettisonable clear

Below left:
The Venom NF2 prototype, G-5-3, was developed as a private venture interim night fighter and the type was later adopted by the RAF.

Below:
The NF2 used the basic Venom single-seat airframe with a two-seat side by side cockpit and AI radar in an extended nose. No 23 Squadron based at Coltishall was the only unit to use the early NF2s.

Bottom:
No 253 Squadron was equipped with the improved Venom NF2As at Waterbeach from April 1955 until August 1957. *J. D. R. Rawlings*

73

view canopies and improvements to the controls including modified fins and rudders as developed during the trials programme. These aircraft were known as NF2As.

The first of these improved aircraft was delivered to No 253 Squadron at Waterbeach on 16 April 1955. The only other units to operate the NF2As were No 219 Squadron formed at Driffield on 5 September 1955 and No 33 Squadron, which joined it the following month. No 33 Squadron only operated the aircraft for 15 months before disbanding in January 1957, followed by No 219 Squadron on 31 July. The last NF2As were withdrawn when No 253 Squadron disbanded at Waterbeach on 31 August 1957.

The Venom NF3 incorporated the NF2A improvements in a new production aircraft in addition to having power operated ailerons, a wholly inset tailplane and improved AI radar. There were still no ejector seats fitted. The prototype NF3, WV928, made its first flight on 22 February 1953 and was followed by 128 production aircraft commencing WX875, 19 from Christchurch, 86 from Chester and 23 from Hatfield. WX786 to WX788 were used by Christchurch for development flying, WX788 being allocated to spinning trials and fitted with an anti-spin parachute. XW786 was delivered to the A&AEE during 1954, WX792 arrived at Boscombe on 8 January 1955, and WX789 was delivered to the de Havilland Engine Co at Hatfield on 25 August 1954. WX790 was used for stalling trials and WX793 for cockpit de-icing development. The first RAF delivery was WX791, which was flown from Christchurch to No 48 MU on 29 March 1955.

NF3s entered service with No 141 Squadron at Coltishall in June 1955, and No 23 Squadron, commanded by Wg Cdr P. L. Chilton DSO, DFC,

Left:
Venom NF2As were used by No 219 Squadron at Driffield from September 1955 until July 1957.
Eric Taylor

Below left:
The NF3 prototype, WV928, was built at Christchurch. It had a number of improvements, but no ejector seats.

Below:
The production standard NF3 had a clear view canopy without ejector seats, and the tailplane extensions removed.

exchanged its NF2s for NF3s three months later.
Three other Venom night fighter units were
formed; No 89 Squadron on 15 December 1955
and No 125 Squadron early the following year to
make up the Stradishall wing; and No 151
Squadron at Leuchars in June 1957, which
re-equipped when most of the other squadrons had
disposed of their Venoms.

The Venom NF3s at Coltishall were replaced by
Javelins from March 1957. The Stradishall wing
began to run down its Venom operations when
No 125 Squadron disbanded on 10 May 1957, and
the last of No 89 Squadron's Venoms had departed
by early 1958. No 151 Squadron remained at
Leuchars until disbanded on 18 September 1961.

One export sale of the Venom night fighter,
known as the NF51, was made. On 16 September
1952 the Swedish Government announced an
order for 62 NF51s, known at J.33s in Swedish
service. The aircraft were built at Chester and by
Fairey at Ringway, the Swedish licence-built
Ghost engines being shipped to the production
lines. The serial numbers allocated were 33001 to
33062, and deliveries took place from 11 December 1952 until 15 July 1957. The early aircraft were
delivered to NF2 standard, but by the end of
production they were up to NF3 standard; the
earlier aircraft were also modified. The Venoms
became the principal night fighters in the
Flygvapret during 1955 and were operated by three
squadrons based at the night fighter wing at
Vasteras. Four of these Venoms were retained
after retirement from combat duty for high speed
target towing, operated by Swedair from Visdel.
They had civil registrations, one example being
SE-DCD.

Now only one relatively complete Venom night
fighter remains, NF3 WX853 at the Mosquito
Aircraft Museum at Salisbury Hall. It served with
No 23 Squadron and is currently being restored,
having been parked in the open for many years.

10
Venoms With Hooks

The Sea Venom was an adaptation of the Venom night fighter airframe intended to achieve the best possible performance out of the design, as an interim naval all-weather fighter to fill the gap between the piston-engined Sea Hornet and the introduction of the more sophisticated Sea Vixen. The design team, led by W. A. Tamblin, was based at the old Airspeed factory at Christchurch to avoid the overcrowding at Hatfield where much effort was going into the Comet jet airliner.

The original prototype Venom NF2, WP227, was evaluated by the Fleet Air Arm, and as a result Specification N.107 was issued for a ship-based all-weather fighter resulting in the Sea Venom. The most obvious changes included the provision of upward-folding wings at about half

Above:
The Sea Venom prototype WK376 was fitted with an arrester hook, but retained the old canopy and fin and rudder shape.

Below:
Sea Venom FAW21 WM574 was fitted with enlarged blown flaps for trials at RAE Bedford.

Above left:
Blown flap Sea Venom WM574 was also used for trials on HMS *Ark Royal* in April 1956, with its approach speeds much reduced.

Left:
The prototype Sea Venom FAW21, XA539, made its maiden flight from the grass at Christchurch on 21 May 1954.

Below left:
Sea Venom prototype WK376 made an initial series of deck trials on HMS *Eagle* in May 1952.

Above:
The ultimate Sea Venom development was the FAW22 with a more powerful Ghost engine. Earlier aircraft were retrofitted. This is development aircraft XG612 photographed over the Needles.

chord to save stowage space on the carrier, a V-frame arrester hook normally stowed above the jet pipe, and the pick-up hooks for the catapult strops. Power came from a 4,850lb thrust Ghost 103 engine.

Three prototypes were ordered, the first two, WK376 and WK379, being built in the Experimental Department at Hatfield, and the third, WK385, at Christchurch. WK376 first flew from Hatfield on 19 April 1951 and was delivered one month later to the A&AEE at Boscombe Down; it commenced carrier trials on 9 July from HMS *Illustrious*. The second aircraft was delivered to Boscombe on 19 September 1952, while the third prototype was the first to be fitted with folding wings and made its first flight from Christchurch on 26 July 1952.

Production then commenced at Christchurch and Chester. The first aircraft, WM500, flew on 27 March 1953 from Christchurch and was initially allocated to company trials. It was followed by WM501 and WM502 which were both used for control assessment at the A&AEE in mid-1954. WM503 and WM507 to WM510 were all used for development flying at Christchurch and WM504 was flown on further deck trials by day and night in October and November 1953. In the following March it was used for rocket assisted take-off (RATO) installation.

Boscombe Down assessed the FAA's first two-seat all-weather jet fighter, with a strike capability, as having excellent deck take-off and landing characteristics, but poor arrester hook damping.

The production aircraft featured increased fin area with dorsal fairings, the reshaped rudder as used on later RAF Venoms, folding wings with non-jettisonable tip fuel tanks, boundary layer fences, a camera gun under the port wing root, symmetrical cast perspex cockpit canopy with underwater jettison capability and a venom FB1 elevator. Boscombe Down insisted on the fitment of a windscreen wiper to keep spray clear, and warned against unduly high stalling speeds in production aircraft. Lateral and directional control characteristics were considered unsuitable for deck landings using standard techniques, but landings in conjunction with the new mirror deck landing aid appeared more promising.

A total of 50 Sea Venom FAW20s were produced, finishing with WM567 which first flew on 6 June 1955. The first FAA unit to be equipped was 890 Squadron which exchanged its Attackers for Sea Venoms at Yeovilton on 20 March 1954, commanded by Lt-Cdr A. G. Johnson. Four aircraft had been delivered in time for their first public appearance at Yeovilton Navy Day on 22 May. After becoming fully equipped and operational following training, a four-aircraft aerobatic team led by the Commanding Officer was formed during the summer of 1955. The Squadron then began deck operations while taking part in Exercise 'Beware'.

During this period afloat serious problems arose which led to the withdrawal of the FAW20 from front-line operations. The arrester hook had insufficient strength to cope with some of the high loads, and was breaking on contact with the wire. This often resulted in a headlong dive into the sea off the ship's bows as there was insufficient time to open up power and go around again. The CO and his observer are reported to have experienced this twice, and waited in their sinking aircraft until the pounding ship's propellers had passed overhead, before making their escape. At this stage no ejector seats were fitted.

On returning to Yeovilton 890 Squadron was renumbered 766 Holding Squadron on 18 October 1955, tasked with providing jet flying practice to pilots and observers who had completed, or were about to join, the all-weather course at No 238 OCU at North Luffenham. The unit was equipped with eight FAW20s and eight of the newer FAW21s. A temporary move was made to Merryfield between 24 November 1956 and 20 January 1957, while the runways at Yeovilton were being extended. By this time it had been named the All-Weather Flying School with responsibility for the all-weather training of pilots and observers for the Fleet Air Arm. On 22 October 1959 the first Sea Vixen arrived; when joined by more, the unit was formed into 766B Flight in May 1960. The Sea Venom was retired from 766 Squadron a year after the first Sea Vixen arrived.

Despite the problems experienced with the early Sea Venoms, two more units were equipped with the aircraft to give them jet operating experience. No 809 Squadron exchanged its all-weather Sea Hornets for Sea Venom FAW20s in May 1954, followed by 891 Squadron, which received its first two aircraft, WM552 and WM549, on 12 November.

While training continued a number of much needed improvements were being made to the Sea Venom, resulting in the FAW21, the naval equivalent of the RAF NF3. These modifications included power-operated ailerons, a long-stroke

Right:
Accessibility for maintenance was very good on the Sea Venom, particularly for the Ghost engine and radar equipment.

Above left:
The Sea Venom was used for the early development of the Firestreak air-to-air heat seeking dog-fight missile. XG662 was one of the aircraft involved in trials.

Left:
Sea Venoms first entered service with 890 Squadron at Yeovilton, but were soon withdrawn to shore training duties because of problems with the arrester hooks. *C. E. Brown*

Below left:
No 891 Squadron Sea Venoms were used for air-to-ground rocket attacks in Operation 'Damon' in Aden against Yemeni rebels in 1960. *Roger Young*

Above:
Sea Venoms of 892 Squadron were embarked abroad HMS *Eagle*, WW187 being an example. *FAA Museum*

undercarriage to absorb more effectively the high landing loads, provision for RATOG and provision for the fitment of the Martin-Baker Mk 4 ejector seats for both crewmen. (In addition all the aircraft built initially without the seats had them fitted at RNAS Stretton in 1957.) Power was from a 4,950lb thrust Ghost 104 engine, which was later replaced by the 5,300lb thrust Ghost 105 in the ultimate FAW22 version. Maxaret non-skid brakes were also fitted, and the arrester hook was strengthened.

The prototype FAW21, XA539, first flew on 21 May 1954, although first production aircraft WM568 had flown from Christchurch one month before on 22 April. A total of 167 FAW21s were built for the FAA, 99 at Chester and 68 at Christchurch.

The prototype was used for carrier trials during August and September 1954 and the aircraft was assessed as suitable for day and night deck operations, if a suitable twin-pointer, open scale air speed indicator was fitted. Four pilots flew XA539 during the trials on HMS *Albion* which consisted of 20 catapult take-offs and landings by day. All landings were made using the mirror aid, and an interim 5° angled deck fitted to the ship made overshooting safe.

Development flying at Christchurch used a number of the early production FAW21s, including WM569 and WM571 to WM575. WM569 later went to Boscombe Down, and WM570 was also delivered to Boscombe on 8 January 1955 for Controller Aircraft (CA) acceptance flying. The first production aircraft operated from the RAE Bedford in late 1956, but crashed near Yeovilton on 3 February 1960 when in service with 738 Squadron based at Lossiemouth. WM574 was allocated to flap blowing development to reduce the approach speed, later going to RAE Bedford to continue the research. It then operated with the ETPS before serving with 831 Squadron at Culdrose and Watton.

The last production FAW21 was XG680, which was later converted to FAW22 standard. It first flew on 21 September 1956 and was deliverd to RNAS Stretton on 4 October. Thirty-nine FAW22s were built commencing XG681, which first flew on 1 October 1956 from Chester and was delivered to Stretton on 2 November. The last Sea Venom FAW22 for the FAA was XG737, which was delivered from Chester to Stretton on 7 January 1958.

By May 1955 both 809 and 891 Squadrons were receiving the first of their FAW21s and were joined by 892 Squadron on 4 July and 893 Squadron in January 1956. No 890 Squadron re-formed with the Sea Venom FAW21s on 6 February 1956 at Yeovilton under the command of Lt-Cdr Brewer, but only lasted until 25 June when it was absorbed by 893 Squadron on HMS *Ark Royal*.

On the nights of 31 October and 1 November 1956 came action for the Sea Venom squadrons and other allied aircraft. Four squadrons operating from off-shore carriers made a number of attacks on Egyptian military installations during the week of the Suez Crisis. By this time 809 Squadron was flying the more powerful FAW22s and shared operations from HMS *Albion* with 892 Squadron, while No 891 and 893 Squadrons operated from HMS *Eagle*. The only FAA casualty was WW284

Top:
A Sea Venom of 809 Squadron appears to require a great deal of manpower to push around the carrier deck. *FAA Museum*

Above:
No 890 Squadron, with a witches emblem, operated Sea Venom FAW21s for only a short while in 1956. *Royal Navy*

Top right:
No 891 Squadron aboard HMS *Ark Royal* used the head of the God 'Kon Tiki' in its squadron badge. *Royal Navy*

Above right:
The compact Sea Venom cockpit had the observer's seat slightly set back on the right-hand side with a radar visor in front.

of 893 Squadron which suffered flak damage, and made a wheels-up landing on the carrier's deck, becoming the first aircraft to be saved by the nylon barrier.

The last front-line unit to equip with Sea Venoms was 894 Squadron, which was commissioned with FAW22s at Merryfield on 14 January 1957. The Squadron performed well during Exercise 'Strikeback' off Norway and in the Arctic Circle during September 1957. Flying from HMS *Eagle* the Squadron made 199 out of an overall total of 860 sorties between 19 and 28 September, thus accounting for nearly 25% of the total sorties without accident, the remainder being flown by the other five participating squadrons.

Action was also seen by 891 Squadron in 1960 during Operation 'Damen' in Aden. Sea Venoms were used in rocket attacks against the Yemeni rebels hidden in the hills. All crews who completed three or more sorties were awarded the campaign medal.

Although the Sea Venom was not designed to carry guided weapons, it proved ideal for development trials of Blue Jay, later to be known as Firestreak. Three aircraft were allocated to this programme — XG607, XG612 (which was also used for FAW22 development) and XG662. No 700 Squadron formed at Ford in 1957 and later Yeovilton to carry out service trials with the new air-to-air weapon, and 893 Squadron received the

three specially modified FAW21s in late 1958 from Christchurch, flown by four of the Squadron pilots. In December the aircraft and crews embarked on HMS *Victorious* and made the first firings by an operational squadron, while working up in the Mediterranean. The targets were pilotless Fireflies from Malta and the Sea Venom pilots scored 80% direct hits, with the remainder near misses. The exercise also was valuable in proving the ship's capability of handling, supply and testing of the Firestreak missiles in preparation for their full time introduction on the Sea Vixen aircraft.

During the 1950s there had been a growing need to use aircraft in the electronic warfare role, early work being undertaken by 751 Squadron at Watton from 1950 as a Naval Development Unit. On 1 May 1958, 831 Squadron was commissioned at Culdrose with Sea Venom FAW21s to take over the task. Initially the Sea Venoms shared operations with Avengers, but these were replaced by Gannets in early 1959, and the later Sea Venom FAW22s began replacing the earlier aircraft in April 1960. The Squadron embarked on HMS *Eagle* to visit Cyprus and Malta, and took part in Exercise 'Barefoot' in November 1959 from HMS *Victorious*. No 831 Squadron then returned to Britain and was based at Watten from the middle of 1963. The unit was finally disbanded there on 16 May 1966, when its work was taken over by the combined RAF/RN No 360 Squadron flying specially modified Canberras.

During the peak of the Sea Venom service, 766

Squadron at Yeovilton was training aircrews in the all-weather fighter and strike syllabus, covering 70 hours flying, of which one-third was at night. Weapons training formed an integral part of the course and included target illumination, interception and navigation exercises at high, medium and low altitudes, covering both ground attack and air-to-air duties. The 10 FAW21s with 766 Squadron flew an average of 45 hours per month. This work was shared at the busiest time by 738 Squadron at Lossiemouth which started adding Sea Venoms to its Sea Hawk complement in January 1958. The unit was responsible for the training of operational flying school students before they joined 766 Squadron. By the middle of 1959 738 Squadron had a dozen Sea Venoms, and the number of Sea Hawks was being reduced. In early 1960 the highest aircrew numbers had passed, and the students reported direct to 766 Squadron for their operational flying training. By the middle of the year all the Sea Venoms had

been replaced with the re-introduction of Sea Hawks with 738 Squadron.

The only other unit to use the Sea Venom was 750 Squadron which first received the aircraft at Hal Far in Malta in July 1960. The main duties of the Squadron were to teach student observers the operation of the radar and navigation of the aircraft in preparation for the Sea Venom squadrons, and later for the Sea Vixen. The flying was almost entirely navigational exercises, roughly one-third at high altitude and the rest at low level. The original four FAW21s were replaced with FAW22s and in July 1965 the Squadron moved to Lossiemouth, increasing its complement to five Sea Venoms, sharing the flying with a number of specially-equipped Sea Princes. With the reduction in the fixed-wing element of the Fleet Air Arm, the need to train naval observers was no longer a requirement. No 750 Squadron was, therefore, disbanded on 24 March 1970 and the Sea Venoms were retired to RNAY Sydenham.

The retirement of the front-line Sea Venoms began when 892 Squadron commissioned with the Sea Vixen at Yeovilton on 2 July 1959 after working up as 700Y Flight. The last carrier-based unit, 894 Squadron, returned from the Far East aboard HMS *Albion* on 17 December 1960 and decommissioned. No 891 Squadron disbanded on 28 July 1961 after flying its last aircraft, XG680 and XG701, to Abbotsinch two days before.

Sea Venoms were also operated by the civilian pilots of Airwork to provide realistic targets for the students of the Air Directors School. Initial operations were with FAW20s from St Davids, a satellite to RNAS Brawdy, from 1955. The first FAW21 arrived in February 1957 and a move was made to Brawdy in October 1958. The aircraft were used for fleet requirements on exercises in air

Above:
FAW22s, of which XG697 was an example, were operated by Airwork at Yeovilton for the Air Director School. *Philip Birtles*

Below:
The Royal Australian Navy ordered 39 Sea Venom

Mk 53s, which operated from HMAS *Melbourne* until early 1970. *RAN*

Bottom:
The initial French version of the Sea Venom was the Aquilon 20, similar to the FAW20. Built by SNCASE it first flew from Marignane on 31 October 1952. *Aerospatiale*

defence, but their primary role was to fly training missions under the control of student air directors, who were being trained to control aircraft by radar while on board ship. The unit moved to Yeovilton in January 1961 and the aircraft was replaced with FAW22s. It was this Airwork unit which was the last to operate the Sea Venom, making the final official flight in XG683 from Yeovilton to Culdrose on 6 October 1970, the aircraft then being allocated to fire practice.

As mentioned earlier, Sea Venom WM574 was used for blown flap research. The aircraft was modified at Christchurch in 1955 to investigate the high lift coefficients when fitted with blown inner flaps of larger chord and span than the standard production aircraft. The Ghost engine was specially adapted to allow high velocity jets of air to flow out of a slot along the top of the flaps. Trials were held initially at RAE Bedford, using the facilities for dummy deck landing, overshoots and catapult take-offs, before joining the Sea Vixen on its carrier trials on HMS *Ark Royal*.

The experimental Sea Venom, with its stalling speed reduced by around 15kt from the standard aircraft, aroused considerable interest during the trials, proving that it had definite advantages. Blown flaps were installed in the Blackburn NA39, later to become the Buccaneer, making the approach of this large aircraft somewhat more docile. Sea Venom WM574 returned to Bedford after the deck trials until joining the ETPS in 1958.

A significant export order for the Sea Venom came from the Royal Australian Navy (RAN) which found the aircraft suited its requirements well. London Order 6970 of 27 February 1956 covered the purchase of 39 FAW53s for service on HMAS *Melbourne*. The FAW53 was developed at Christchurch from the FAW21, with special equipment required by the RAN, and it became the first all-weather jet fighter to serve with a Commonwealth navy.

The first FAW53, WZ893, was delivered to Boscombe Down on 1 March 1955 and was joined by WZ941 on 2 November. WZ894, WZ895 and WZ944 were used for a short while at Christchurch for development flying. All 39 aircraft were built at Christchurch, comprising WZ893 to WZ911 and WZ927 to WZ946, the final aircraft being delivered on 18 January 1956 to RNAS Stretton, like the remainder, before embarking on HMAS *Melbourne* for their journey to Australia.

The first RAN squadron to form was No 808 at Culdrose on 23 August 1955, initially using FAW20s on loan from the FAA to allow training to commence. HMAS *Melbourne* was named at Barrow-in-Furness on 28 October, having been converted from HMS *Majestic,* becoming the flagship of the Australian Fleet.

HMAS *Melbourne* left Portsmouth in March 1956 for Sydney as the most modern aircraft carrier in her class in the world and carried the Sea Venoms of No 808 Squadron, which had embarked on 29 February. The ship was rather crowded, as also on board were the Gannets of Nos 816 and 817 Squadrons.

The Sea Venoms served with No 808 Squadron until 1 December 1958, when No 805 Squadron assumed the all-weather fighter role from 18 August 1958 until 30 June 1963. There was then a lull for just over a year until No 816 Squadron commissioned on 21 July 1964 and continued to operate the Sea Venoms until final retirement on 25 August 1967.

Shore support for the RAN was provided by HMAS *Albatross* at Nowra, New South Wales, and when the squadrons were not at sea, they were based at this airfield. Also resident at Nowra was No 724 Squadron, which was formed on 1 June 1955, as a miscellaneous air squadron. Although it was never fully equipped with Sea Venoms, a number were used for training on shore based duty only.

Many of the surviving Sea Venoms were disposed of through the Australian Department of Supply on 25 July 1966, but at least six were retained in service with No 724 Squadron as late as January 1970 when they were finally withdrawn from use.

As with the Vampire fighter-bombers, the French Government adopted the Sea Venom and modified the type for its needs as the Aquilon. Licence production commenced with Sud Aviation at Marignane near Marseilles with four prototypes to the Sea Venom FAW20 standard, followed by a fifth improved single prototype, known as the Aquilon 201. This was used as the prototype for the Aquilon 202, changes including the installation of ejector seats, a rearward sliding canopy and a strengthened landing gear. A further development was the Aquilon 203 adapted to become a single seat all-weather fighter, fitted with the American APQ 94 radar and a new rearward sliding canopy. The licence production consisted of 25 Aquilon 201s, generally similar to the Sea Venom FAW20, 25 Aquilon 202s and 40 Aquilon 203s. A small number of the Aquilon 201 were later modified to become two-seat all-weather fighter trainers as the Aquilon 204.

The first Aquilon made its maiden flight from Marignane on 31 October 1952 and production aircraft equipped three *flottiles* with the French Navy. The first unit was 16F which received the new aircraft at Hyères Naval Air Base in early 1955. While operating from this base, detachments were sent to Algiers for air policing and the support of ground forces in the Algerian campaign. *Flotille 16F* then embarked on the aircraft carrier *Clemenceau* from 1960 until 1962 and was finally disbanded in 1963. The second unit, *Flotille 11F,* formed at Hyères in mid-1955, soon moving to Bizerta in Tunisia. *11F* also was active in the Algerian operations and embarked on *Clemenceau* until the Aquilons were replaced by Etendards in 1962. The only other unit was *Escadrille 59S,* which was formed as an all-weather fighter training school with Aquilon 203s and 204s from 1958 until 1963. A few Aquilons continued to fly during 1965 until the order grounding the aircraft was received. One is known to survive and is being restored by the Musée de l'Air at Le Bourget.

Below:
Aquilon 201 No 05, F-WGVT was built in France as the prototype of the French equivalent of the Sea Venom FAW21.

Bottom:
The Aquilon 203 was a single-seat development by SNCASE, and is seen aboard the French carrier *Clémenceau.* *E. C. Armées*

11
The DH-110

With the promise indicated by the early navalised Vampires in operation with the Fleet Air Arm, it was decided to investigate an advanced all-weather jet fighter with the security of two engines. Initial discussions commenced between de Havilland and the Admiralty in 1946 resulting in proposals for a project allocated the type number DH.110. The customary twin boom layout was retained to allow easier carrier stowage and keeping the engines as close together as possible to avoid asymmetric controls problems in the event of an engine failure. Wings were swept back at an angle of 40°, as a result of research from the DH.108 development programme, and provision was made for them to fold to allow lowering in the deck lifts and to reduce stowage space. Proposed armament was four of the then new 30mm cannon. A unique

feature was the pilot's cockpit offset to port, while the observer was buried in the fuselage to starboard under a flush-fitting hatch. Small windows were provided in the cockpit side and roof, but the observer was in semi-darkness because of the dimness of the signals on early AI radars.

In January 1947 Naval Specification No 40/46 and RAF Specification F.44/46 were issued to cover basically similar requirements for a night

Below:
The prototype DH.110, WG236, made its first flight from Hatfield in the hands of John Cunningham on 26 September 1951. It crashed at Farnborough on 6 September 1952, killing the two crew and over 20 spectators.

fighter. De Havilland offered the DH.110 for both tasks in navalised and land-based versions respectively. Greater interest was shown by the RAF, which updated the specification to F.4/48 in February 1948. In April 1949 the Ministry of Supply confirmed the interest by ordering from de Havilland seven land-based night fighters and two long-range fighter prototypes for the RAF, together with two of each of the night fighter and strike fighter prototypes for the Fleet Air Arm, to specification N14/49. Meanwhile as a back up for the RAF, four prototypes of the competing delta-winged Gloster, GA.5, were also ordered.

As an example of the advanced nature of the programme at that time, Specification F.44/46 issued on 24 January 1947 called for a prototype night fighter for the RAF, which would be available rapidly and capable of intercepting hostile aircraft at up to 40,000ft. Maximum speed was to be at least 525kt at 25,000ft; it had to be capable of climbing to its service ceiling of 45,000ft in no more than 10 minutes from pressing the starter button at the holding point close to the end of the runway; and it was to have a minimum endurance of two hours including a climb to 25,000ft with 15 minutes of combat and the remainder cruising on patrol. Provision was to be made for the carriage of drop tanks to increase the range.

Very rapid take-off was called for in at most 10 seconds, but preferably in five, without external assistance such as catapults or RATOG. Take-off distance was to be in 1,500yd, with landing in 1,200yd over an imaginery 50ft barrier. Airbrakes were to be fitted and be able to operate in four seconds. While flying at top speed at sea level, the airframe had to be strong enough to withstand up to 4g loads while manoeuvring in evasive or attacking action. The pressure cabin was to be able to reproduce the altitude pressure of 25,000ft at the ceiling 45,000ft.

The workload was such that two crewmen would be carried, a pilot and radar observer, and navigation equipment and aids were to include multi-channel VHF, AI, Rebecca, IFF and possibly a blind-landing capability. Armament was to comprise four forward-firing 30mm cannon with sufficient ammunition for 15 seconds firing per gun, aimed through the gyro gunsight and with radar presentation.

The aircraft was to be capable of economic production of at least 150 at a maximum rate of 10 per month. The cockpit interiors were to be matt black with all emergency controls in red, and the cabin was either to be jettisonable in an emergency, or the crew were to be supplied with ejector seats. Self-sealing tanks were not mandatory, but if hit they should retain at least 50% of the fuel after one strike. Full night flying equipment was required and the crew were provided with oxygen for 2.5 hours at 25,0000ft, and two K-type dinghies together with their parachutes. Simple and rapid servicing was essential for a quick turn-round between sorties.

In November 1949, for financial and political reasons, the Royal Navy selected the less complex and more readily available Sea Venom to replace its Sea Hornets, while the RAF order was reduced to two prototypes each of the DH.110 and GA.5. This seriously delayed the development of both types and demanded the introduction of interim types based on current aircraft to fill the resulting gap.

The two prototype DH.110s were built in the Experimental Department at Hatfield, power coming from a pair of 7,500lb thrust Rolls-Royce Avon RA.7 engines, with the air intakes in the wing root, and the exhaust between the booms and below the high mounted tailplane. The first of these large and impressive aircraft, WG236, made its 46-minute maiden flight in the hands of John Cunningham on 26 September 1951, just too late for that year's SBAC display at Farnborough. During its extensive schedule it exceeded the speed of sound in a shallow dive on 9 April 1952, and was joined by the black painted second prototype WG240 when it flew on 25 July 1952.

Just over a month later the first prototype made its public debut at the Farnborough air show, only to break up when flying fast and low towards the crowd on 6 September. John Derry, the pilot, and his observer, Tony Richards, were both killed when the main portion of the airframe hit the ground, while one of the engines separated and fell in the crowd viewing from the hill, killing 29 spectators and injuring many others. The accident investigation found that the disintegration of WG236 was caused by torsional failure of the wing during a combination of high acceleration and rate of roll, the leading edge wing skins peeling back. The SBAC amended the display rules at Farnborough by banning all flying towards the public enclosures, a commonsense rule which is now in operation at all air shows.

The grounded second prototype was modified by reinforcing the structure with skin doubler plates and the tail outline was revised. Test flying recommenced in the spring of 1953, when it became the first British aircraft with an all-moving tail-plane.

With the loss of RAF interest in the DH.110, and despite development problems and accidents, the Gloster GA.5 was ordered into super-priority production as a land based all-weather fighter, leaving the future of the DH.110 rather bleak.

However, the FAA still had a requirement for a high performance all-weather fighter, and in 1952 a requirement was published for a Sea Venom replacement to be capable of all-weather fighting and strike duties. A swept-wing Venom, known as the DH.116, was considered, but shelved in favour of updating the DH.110 and continuing its development under a Naval contract. The new aircraft was to bear only a superficial resemblance to the original design with power coming from higher thrust Avon engines, increased fuel capacity and the full range of naval modifications. The four cannon were retained as secondary armament, but primary weapons were to be the new Blue Jay — later to become Firestreak — infra-red homing air-to-air missiles. For the first time de Havilland was becoming involved in the complexities of an overall weapon system, rather than an aircraft with stores attached.

The surviving second prototype, WG240, was delivered to Boscombe Down in September 1954 in preparation for initial deck trials. These were completed as a series of touch-and-go landings, as no arrester hook was fitted, on HMS *Albion* on 23 September, flown by Lt-Cdr J. Elliott. For these trials a strengthened undercarriage was fitted and later the aircraft was fitted with four missile launch pylons below the inboard wing.

Development continued with the order in February 1954 for a semi-navalised DH.110 prototype Mk 20X, XF828. It was built at the old airspeed factory at Christchurch, to where all design activity, led by Mr W. A. Tamblin, had been transferred. The more powerful Rolls-Royce Avon 208 engines developing 11,230lb of thrust each were fitted, as well as arrester gear and a long stroke undercarriage. However, radar was not installed and the wings did not fold. First flight was from Christchurch to Hurn on 20 June 1955, piloted by Jock Elliott, who by this time was in charge of the DH110 flight development programme. The first deck landings were carried out on board HMS *Ark Royal* on 5 April 1956 by Cdr S. G. Orr, the programme including unassisted and steam catapult take-offs and arrested landings under all operating conditions.

On completion of the flight test programme XF828 was delivered to the RAE Bedford before allocation to ground towing training at the School of Aircraft Handling at Culdrose on 28 November 1960, when its outer wings were cut off. It was finally relegated in a battered state to fire practice in June 1970 and was soon destroyed.

Top right:
WG240 was later modified to represent as close as possible the Sea Vixen production shape, including a pointed radome and cut-back fin trailing edge.

Centre right:
The third prototype DH.110, XF828, was partially navalised with an arrester hook, but remained without folding wings. It carried the pitot tube for test purposes.

Below right:
XF828 was used for deck trials on HMS *Ark Royal* in April 1956 when a series of catapult launches were made. Note the strop dropping away.

94

12

The Sea Vixen

The long-awaited initial production order for the DH.110 was placed in January 1955, covering a total of 78 aircraft including a batch of 21 pre-production aircraft to be used in the development of all aspects of this complicated weapons system. By this means production would be rapidly established and the introduction into service would be as soon as possible.

The airframe was about 80% redesigned, to specification N.139P, and power was from a pair of Avon 208 engines developing 10,000lb thrust each. Major changes to the aircraft included hydraulically-operated folding wings, a new cockpit canopy for the pilot, catapult pick-up points, a steerable nosewheel and the latest AI radar housed under a pointed radome. A large ventral airbrake was fitted and improvements to the airframe included increased tail-boom clearance and cut-backs on the fin trailing edge to reduce the length. The radome could be folded sideways to further reduce length and allow servicing. The Avon engines were fitted from the top of the fuselage, rather than below as in the prototypes.

The DH.110 was the first British jet fighter not to be armed with guns, as provision for cannons was deleted and the Firestreak became the prime armament, four being carried on underwing pylons. In addition, 28 2in rocket projectiles were stowed in a retractable ventral pack just forward and to either side of the nosewheel. Additional war loads such as bombs, rocket packs or fuel tanks could be carried on underwing pylons.

On 5 March 1957 the DH.110 was officially designated Sea Vixen FAW Mk 20, later amended to Sea Vixen FAW Mk 1. The first production aircraft, XJ474, was rolled out in February 1957 at Christchurch (where the production line was established) and made its maiden flight on 20 March to the flight test department at nearby Hurn, where the airfield facilities were more suited to high performance aircraft.

The first production aircraft was allocated to handling trials at Boscombe Down, inluding flutter checks, and during 1957 undertook deck acceptance trials including steam-catapult launches, on HMS *Ark Royal*, with more launches following in

1962. In 1961 it was used for spinning trials, for which it was fitted with an anti-spin parachute, and finished up at the RAE Bedford with the Naval Flight on arrester hook bounce trials in March 1963. XJ474 was 'put out to grass', in the early 1970s and was scrapped by 1976.

The second production aircraft, XJ475, first flew on 28 June 1957 and was the engineering development aircraft used for systems testing at Hatfield. It was also used for performance measurements from mid-1958 to late 1959. From August 1962 until 1964 this aircraft was used on Red Top missile development as a non-destructive target for XN685. The new clear-view canopy installation was carried out in 1964 followed by generator trials the next year. The aircraft was passed to Hawker Siddeley Dynamics in August 1965 and remained in the company's charge until departure to Boscombe Down on 19 October 1968. It was scrapped at Boscombe by March 1971.

XJ476 was originally allocated to radar and sighting trials at the A&AEE. It was then painted white overall for guided weapons trials on the Woomera ranges in Australia and shipped out with XJ481 on 13 March 1960. Both aircraft returned to Hatfield in March 1963, XJ476 continuing on guided weapons trials mainly as a radar target for Red Top development. It replaced XJ475 at the A&AEE from 1970 until at least 1973.

XJ477 was used for armament trials at the A&AEE in early 1960, in particular rocket

Right, top to bottom:
The Sea Vixen was fitted with a large under-fuselage air-brake. FAW1 XJ474 was the first production aircraft.

Sea Vixen FAW1 XJ476 was painted white for weapons trials at Woomera in Australia. *Philip Birtles*

Sea Vixen FAW1 XJ481 also was used for Firestreak trials at Woomera and later missile development at Hatfield. It is now preserved by the FAA Museum at Yeovilton. *Philip Birtles*

After trials with the RN XJ474 was used by C Squadron, A&AEE for further deck trials on HMS *Ark Royal*.

sighting, having undertaken carrier trials on HMS *Centaur* the previous year. Following its trials programme the aircraft joined 766 Squadron at Yeovilton on 8 August 1962 until retired to Arbroath in 1967 as instructional airframe A2601. XJ478 was used for Firestreak development before being delivered to 766 Squadron at Yeovilton in 1962, where it crashed during mirror deck landing training on 8 March 1965, killing both crew when control was lost on a down-wind turn. XJ479 was sent to Libya on tropical trials, but crashed there on 28 October 1958 after bird ingestion into the engines. It was replaced by XJ485 in August 1959.

XJ480 was used to check radio and navigation equipment at RAE Bedford in 1959 and was also used for engine development. It served with 899 and finally 766 Squadron, becoming an aerobatic mount in the 'Fred's Five' team from 1962 until 1966. Before going to Woomera XJ481 undertook carrier trials on HMS *Centaur* in 1959, as well as FAA handling trials. On return from Australia it was flown on missile development trials during 1963, progressing to TV trials during the following two years, all the time being based at Hatfield. For these latter trials the usual radome was replaced by a nose cone fitted with an optically flat glass panel at the forward end, protecting the TV camera. The

aircraft left for Boscombe Down in November 1968 and remained there until retired to the Fleet Air Arm Museum at Yeovilton in 1974. It is currently stored in the open near the Museum buildings.

Cold weather trials were undertaken by XJ482 in the climatic chamber at Weybridge in July 1959. It became the first aircraft with 700Y Flight for service trials when it was delivered to Yeovilton on 3 November 1958. It became a 766 Squadron aircraft from 1962, being used as one of the mounts for 'Fred's Five', and was retired to Lee-on-Solent in 1969. Following a move to Flight Refuelling at Tarrant Rushton in 1972, the aircraft was acquired

Below:
FAW1 XJ474 was operated by the RN Test Squadron for carrier trials.

Below right:
Sea Vixens were capable of 'buddy' flight refuelling using an underwing pod. These are two FAW2s of 899 Squadron. *Royal Navy*

Bottom right:
The FAW1 could carry a Martin Bullpup as an underwing store.

for preservation by the Norfolk Aircraft Museum in 1980. XJ483 took part in the final deck trials on HMS *Victorious*, flew on cabin air conditioning trials and joined 700Y Flight at Yeovilton. It finally entered FAA service with 890 Squadron on 3 August 1962. Additional aircraft used by 700Y Flight for service trials were XJ484, XJ486, XJ487 and XJ489.

As already mentioned, XJ485 flew on tropical trials, replacing XJ479, and on return was allocated to RAE Bedford. It later served with 766 Squadron, to whom it was delivered on 30 June 1960, but was allocated to Red Top weapons trials at Hatfield in 1962. It was back at Bedford in the early 1970s. Following trials with 700Y Flight, both XJ486 and XJ487 joined 892 Squadron at Yeovilton and aboard HMS *Ark Royal*, ending up as instructional airframes at Lee-on-Solent and Arbroath respectively.

Flight refuelling trials were flown by XJ488 using the 'buddy' technique of carrying its own flight refuelling pod under the wing instead of the normal fuel tank, so that the hose could be reeled out to top up another Sea Vixen or any other combat aircraft fitted with the probe. Mock-up boom fairings were fitted for Mk 2 aerodynamic tests. This aircraft was used for systems and weapons development for many years, including engine performance in mid-1961, LOX (liquid oxygen) trials in March 1962, and RRE Pershore trials with the radar until August 1962, when it was delivered to Hatfield for Red Top computer trials starting in November 1963. A new RT system was tested in 1964 and then a busy programme of PR, Bullpup and LABS (low altitude bombing system) development started in January 1965, first at Bedford and then Boscombe. It joined C Squadron at the A&AEE on 18 October 1967 and was painted black overall in 1968. It was finally relegated to fire practice in 1973 at Boscombe. XJ492 served briefly at Boscombe Down before delivery to 892 Squadron. XJ494, the last pre-production aircraft, was used by the A&AEE for LABS bombing technique development from April 1959 until 1962. It later served with 899 Squadron after conversion to Mk 2 before flying from Hatfield in early 1971 on Martel trials, continuing these at Boscombe.

The 'buddy' refuelling trials with XJ488 were shared with XJ516, which also flew on deck trials aboard HMS *Victorious* in October 1959. XJ526 was used on bombing and sighting trials at Boscombe and Bedford before entering squadron service, and XJ560 was used for Del Mar target tug

Above left:
The Sea Vixen FAW2 prototype was XN684 converted from a Mk 1 with pinion fuel tanks and armed with Red Top air-to-air missiles.

Left:
No 892 Squadron was the first to be commissioned with Sea Vixens, at Yeovilton on 2 July 1959.

Below left:
No 892 Squadron embarked on HMS *Hermes* under the command of Cdr J. Petrie. *FAA Museum*

Above:
This Sea Vixen FAW1 of 893 Squadron was forced to use the nylon crash barrier on HMS *Ark Royal* when its starboard undercarriage failed to lock down.
FAA Museum

Below:
No 890 Squadron was the headquarters squadron based at Yeovilton and responsible for the investigation of operational techniques. *Philip Birtles*

Bottom:
FAW1 XN654 of 893 Squadron aboard HMS *Victorious*. *FAA Museum*

development at Hatfield and Boscombe from 1962 until 1964. XJ564 also went on tropical trials and served with C Squadron at Boscombe from 1962 on sighting trials and engine development until conversion to Mk 2 standard in 1964. XJ582 was allocated to Bullpup missile development at Hatfield, together with photo reconnaisance pod development, followed by bombing trials at Boscombe in 1963. Further photo reconnaissance pod trials were carried out with XN700 at Boscombe in 1963.

Two aircraft, XN684 and XN685, were taken from the Christchurch production lines and converted to the Mk 2 prototypes at Hatfield, but more of that version shortly. Production of the Sea Vixen at Christchurch ceased with the 118th aircraft, XN710, which first flew on 10 August 1962, although the last aircraft to leave the airfield was XN705, which was delivered on 31 October the same year. The production was then transferred to Chester where a single Mk 1 (XP918) was produced before changing to the Mk 2s, of which 29 were built; the last one, XS590, made its first flight on 3 February 1966.

Following the intensive service trials in which 700Y Flight led by Cdr M. H. J. Petrie RN used a total of eight Sea Vixen Mk 1s, the unit was re-formed and commissioned on 2 July 1959 as 892 Squadron. This initial unit embarked on HMS Ark Royal on 3 March 1960 for sea trials and transferred to HMS Victorious later in the year. A move was then made to HMS Hermes, before the Squadron joined HMS Centaur in December 1963 for operations in Indonesia, Radfan and Dar-es-Salaam.

In November 1959 operational and conversion training became the responsibility of 766 Squadron at Yeovilton, which received its full quota of Sea Vixen Mk 1s by September 1980. It was instructors from this squadron who formed the aerobatic team 'Fred's Five', which performed for a number of airshow seasons.

The formation of operational squadrons continued when 890 Squadron, commanded by Lt-Cdr W. H. Hart, commissioned at Yeovilton on 1 February 1960. After serving briefly on the newly commissioned HMS Hermes in July 1960, 890 Squadron joined HMS Ark Royal, aboard which all sea-going operations were conducted by this unit.

No 893 Squadron was commissioned on 9 September 1960 and embarked on HMS Ark Royal for participation in NATO exercises in the Norwegian Sea and 10 days of cold weather operational trials in the Davis Strait. When moved to HMS Centaur, the Squadron was active in the Kuwait crisis.

Formed as the Sea Vixen Mk 1 Headquarters Squadron, 899 was commissioned at Yeovilton on 1 February 1961 to evaluate new operational ideas and maintain the standards of the service units.

With the Sea Vixen Mk 1s in production and entering service, de Havillands was investigating a range of improvements and developments of the basic aircraft to increase the range and performance in general. To achieve the increase in endurance the Avon engines were to be replaced by 11,380lb thrust Rolls-Royce Spey engines. Additional fuel could be carried in a pair of fixed 250gal wing tip fuel tanks, plus a 850gal fuel tank behind the cockpit in a lengthened fuselage. To improve performance, both at the top end of the scale and on the approach to carrier decks, reheats were considered for the engines and flap blowing. An even more advanced proposeal was for a thin-wing supersonic aircraft with a maximum speed of Mach 1.4 to Specification F.153D, also being competed for by the thin-wing Gloster Javelin. Although the Javelin was successful initially, the complete programme was cancelled.

In the early 1960s a more conservative improvement programme was initiated involving

the installation of additional pinion fuel tanks ahead of the tail booms, and the missile armament changed to the improved Red Top air-to-air missile. Any additional equipment was installed in the enlarged boom fairings behind the fuel tanks. The new development was designated the Sea Vixen FAW Mk 2 and, as already noted, XN684 and XN685 were the initial conversions at Hatfield. The first aircraft was flown as a Mk 2 by Chris Capper on 1 June 1962, followed by XN685 on 17 August. Both aircraft were allocated to development, in particular Red Top trials at Hatfield and Boscombe Down with No 13 Joint Service Trials Unit (13 JSTU), where they were delivered in July and April 1964 respectively. The JSTU trials were completed in February 1966 and both aircraft were delivered to Chester for full conversion to Mk 2 service standard before joining 893 Squadron on HMS *Hermes* in 1968. XN684 eventually made the last Sea Vixen deck landing

while serving with 899 Squadron on HMS *Eagle*, before returning to Yeovilton on 23 January 1972 to decommission. The aircraft joined a number of others on the Sydenham scrap heap in February 1973.

The first production Sea Vixen Mk 2, XP919, made its maiden flight from Chester on 8 March 1963, and in addition to the new build aircraft, the majority of surviving Mk 1s were converted to Mk 2 standard at Chester and Sydenham. XP919 went to Bedford for deck landing trials, flew with the full load of four Red Tops and was used for CA release at Boscombe in late 1963. It flew on performance trials at Hatfield in 1964 and Boscombe from March 1965, including auto throttle development, and it made the first firing of the full load of 144 unguided rockets on 6 August 1964. It went to Bedford again in July 1965 for use on LABS/Bullpup assessment and returned to Boscombe on 23 March 1966. With its trials flying

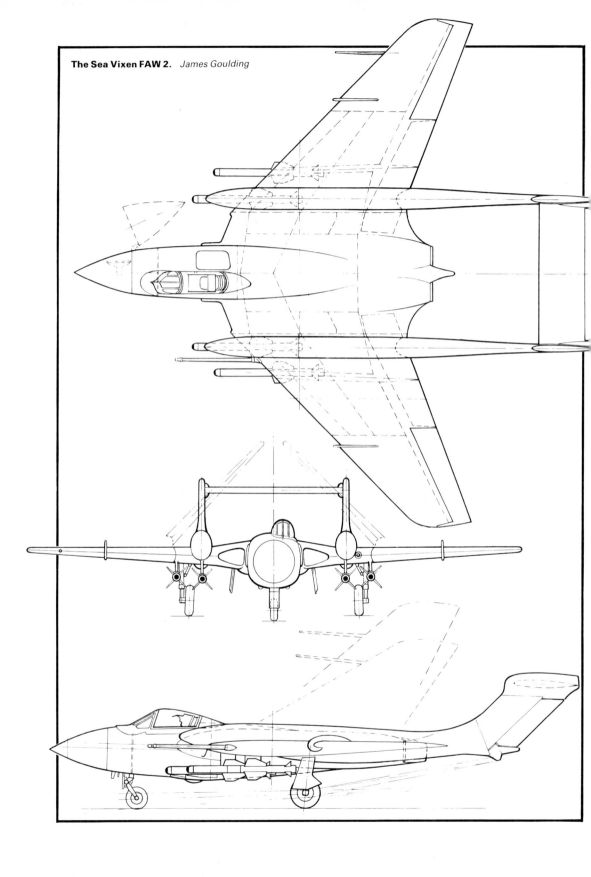

The Sea Vixen FAW 2. *James Goulding*

Top:
A Bullpup-armed FAW2 of 899 Squadron on the steam catapult aboard HMS *Eagle*. *FAA Museum*

Above:
For training purposes small practice bombs were carried by 766 Squadron Sea Vixen FAW2s on the underwing pylons. Here XN687 is being prepared for a practice bombing sortie. *Philip Birtles*

This picture:
No 899 Squadron operated the FAW2 from HMS *Eagle*. *FAA Museum*

completed XP919 served with 766 Squadron from 1968 until transfer to 890 Squadron in 1971, both at Yeovilton. It was retired to Abingdon on 2 August 1971 for service at Halton as ground instruction airframe 8163M, but was acquired for preservation on 23 June 1975 by Leisure Sport at Chertsey, which disposed of the aircraft to the Norwich Air Museum on 25 August 1981.

Sea Vixen Mk 2 XP920 was used for armament service trials, including Lepus flares, in 1963. It was delivered to Boscombe on 24 January 1964 for bombing trials, operating from HMS *Hermes* from February to April. Catapult trials were undertaken at Bedford in September 1964, the aircraft returning to Hatfield before going to Boscombe again on 15 October 1965 where it was used for frangible hatch development in 1969, being recognisable by a bulged observer's entry hatch allowing ejection straight through. The aircraft served with 892 Squadron, but was eventually one

of the few conversions to a U3 drone at Llanbedr in 1975.

Service deliveries commenced with XP921 to the Aircraft Handling Unit at Brawdy on 13 August 1963, 899 Squadron being the first to equip with the FAW2s, replacing its Mk 1s. XJ580 returned to Chester to become the first production Mk 2 conversion of a total of 67 by June 1968.

No 899 Squadron continued to be the Yeovilton-based headquarters squadron, introducing the new version of the Sea Vixen into service. In December of 1964 the Squadron embarked on HMS *Eagle* and participated in the Rhodesian blockade until returning to Yeovilton in August 1966. To continue the training task, 766 Squadron received its first Mk 2, XS582, on 7 July 1965, while 893 Squadron began re-equipment on 4 November 1965. No 890 Squadron disbanded in 1966, but recommissioned in September 1967 as the new headquarters squadron, initially using four Sea

Above left:
In later service the FAW2s were fitted with a frangible hatch over the observer's cockpit for ejection straight through. This is XJ526 of 893 Squadron at Yeovilton in 1969. *Philip Birtles*

Left:
No 899 Squadron was the last FAA unit to operate the Sea Vixen on board a carrier, returning to Yeovilton on 23 January 1972 for disbandment. XN684, a FAW2, carried unofficial 'artwork' when preparing for take-off from HMS *Eagle* during final disembarkation. *FAA Museum*

Above:
FAW2 XN653 was retained by RAE Bedford until 1976 and carried the RAF fin flash. *Philip Birtles*

Vixen Mk 1s, but later converting to Mk 2s as they became available. No 892 Squadron re-equipped with the Mk 2s during 1963, joining HMS *Hermes* in time to participate in the Aden crisis. A return was made to Yeovilton in February 1968, when the Squadron formed the FAA aerobatic team consisting of five aircraft known as 'Simon's Circus'.

The departure of the Sea Vixen from service commenced with the disbandment of 892 Squadron in October 1968 in preparation for the entry into service of the Phantom FG1 the following April. No 893 Squadron disbanded on the return of HMS *Hermes* to Portsmouth in July 1970, 10 of its aircraft going to RNAY Sydenham for storage pending any decision on the future size of the FAA. They were scrapped with many of the surviving Sea Vixens between 1971 and 1973.

With the disbandment of 766 Squadron at Yeovilton on 10 December 1970, the training task and some of its aircraft passed to 890 Squadron. In turn the 890 Squadron aircraft were passed to the Airwork-operated Fleet Requirements Unit (FRU) at Yeovilton. No 890 Squadron itself finally disbanded on 6 August 1971 as the last land-based FAA Sea Vixen unit, three of its aircraft having been delivered to Cranwell for ground instruction

three days previously. No 899 Squadron remained on HMS *Eagle* until returning to Yeovilton on 23 January 1972 for disbandment. Five of its aircraft were delivered to Llanbedr for drone conversion, while others went to Farnborough for storage and drone preparation.

The Farnborough-based programme consisted mainly of removing unwanted equipment and preparing the aircraft for flying to Flight Refuelling Ltd at Tarrant Rushton where conversion to U3 drones took place. Funding for this programme was always short, the work on the programme petering out with a mere handful of conversions completed, some still being around at Hurn in 1984, mainly up for disposal. The Sea Vixens continued in service with the FRU at Yeovilton until they too were withdrawn in January 1974, one or two aircraft remaining as flyable hacks at Bedford and Sydenham for the remainder of the year.

Amongst the aircraft preserved is Mk 2 conversion XJ565 at the Mosquito Aircraft Museum. As a Mk 1 it served with 766, 892 and 893 Squadrons, before conversion to Mk 2 standard between July 1965 and February 1967. It joined 899 Squadron on 13 Febuary 1967 and was retired to the AHU at Brawdy on 2 December 1968. One year later it was delivered to the RAE Bedford for non-flying catapult and arrester trials, completing 117 arrests between 20 February 1970 and 10 August 1973. It languished at Bedford until struck off charge on 29 July 1976 before being acquired by the Mosquito Aircraft Museum which collected it on 31 October. This aircraft is being restored to the markings of 899 Squadron.

The Sea Vixen therefore closes the era of de Havilland jet fighters. Although it failed to achieve an RAF order, in favour of the Gloster Javelin, the smaller number built remained in service longer. The Sea Vixen was an effective ground-attack aircraft, while also being capable of a rapid climb to 40,000ft where it could out-turn many interceptors.

Appendices

1 Vampire Specifications

Mark	Powerplant	Span	Length	Height	Wing area
Prototypes	One 2,700lb thrust Goblin 1	40ft	30ft 9in	9ft	266sq ft
F Mk 1	One 3,100lb thrust Goblin 1	40ft	30ft 9in	8ft 10in	266sq ft
F Mk 1*	One 4,400lb thrust Ghost 2/2	48ft	30ft 9in	8ft 10in	
F Mk II & IV	One 4,500lb thrust Nene 1	40ft	30ft 9in	8ft 10in	266sq ft
F Mk 3	One 3,100lb thrust Goblin 2	40ft	30ft 9in	8ft 10in	266sq ft
F Mk 5	One 3,100lb thrust Goblin 2	38ft	30ft 9in	8ft 10in	262sq ft
FB Mk 6	One 3,350lb thrust Goblin 3	38ft	30ft 9in	8ft 10in	262sq ft
FB Mk 9	One 3,350lb thrust Goblin 3	38ft	30ft 9in	8ft 10in	262sq ft
NF Mk 10	One 3,350lb thrust Goblin 3	38ft	34ft 7in	6ft 7in	261sq ft
T Mk 11	One 3,500lb thrust Goblin 35	38ft	34ft 6.5in	6ft 2in	262sq ft
F Mk 20	One 3,100lb thrust Goblin 2	38ft	30ft 9in	8ft 10in	262sq ft
FB Mk 30	One 5,000lb thrust Nene 2-VH	38ft	30ft 9in	8ft 10in	262sq ft
FB Mk 50 & 52	One 3,350lb thrust Goblin 3	38ft	30ft 9in	8ft 10in	262sq ft
FB Mk 51 & 53	One 5,000lb thrust Nene 102B	38ft	30ft 9in	8ft 10in	262sq ft

* Mk 1 TG278 for high altitude Ghost engine development.

Mark	Empty wt	All-up wt	Max speed	Initial climb	Ceiling	Range
F Mk 1	6,372lb	10,480lb	540mph	4,300ft/min		730 miles
F Mk 3	7,134lb	11,970lb	531mph	4,350ft/min	43,500ft	1,145 miles
FB Mk 5	7,253lb	12,360lb	535mph	4,050ft/min	40,000ft	1,170 miles
FB Mk 6	7,283lb	12,390lb	548mph	4,800ft/min		1,220 miles
FB Mk 9	7,283lb	12,390lb	548mph	4,800ft/min		1,220 miles
NF Mk 10	6,984lb	13,100lb	538mph	4,500ft/min		1,220 miles
T Mk 11	7,380lb	11,150lb	538mph	4,500ft/min	40,000ft	840 miles
F Mk 20	7,623lb	12,660lb	526mph	4,300ft/min	43,500ft	1,140 miles
FB Mk 30	7,600lb	11,000lb	570mph	4,500ft/min	49,000ft	
FB Mk 53	7,656lb	12,628lb	568mph	4,500ft/min	44,000ft	

2 Venom Specifications

Mark	Powerplant	Span	Length	Height	Wing area
FB Mk 1 & 4	One 4,850lb thrust Ghost 103	41ft 8in	31ft 10in	6ft 2in	279.75sq ft
NF Mk 2 & FAW Mk 20	One 4,850lb thrust Ghost 103	42ft 11in	33ft 1in	7ft 7in	279.75sq ft
NF Mk 3 & FAW Mk 21	One 4,950lb thrust Ghost 104	42ft 11in	36ft 7in	6ft 6in	279.75sq ft
FAW Mk 22	One 5,300lb thrust Ghost 105	42ft 11in	36ft 7in	8ft 6.25in	279.75sq ft
FAW Mk 53	One 5,300lb thrust Ghost 104	42ft 11in	36ft 7in	8ft 8.25in	279.75sq ft
Aquilon	One 4,840lb thrust Ghost 48	42ft 11in	—	—	279.75sq ft

Mark	All-up wt	Max speed	Initial climb	Ceiling	Range
FB Mk 1 & 4	15,400lb	640mph	9,000ft/min		
NF Mk 2 &					
FAW Mk 20					
NF Mk 3 &					
FAW Mk 21		630mph	8,762ft/min	49,200ft	1,000 miles
FAW Mk 22	15,800lb	575mph	5,900ft/min	40,000ft	705 miles
FAW Mk 53	15,800lb	587mph	8,762ft/min	49,200ft	1,000 miles

3 Sea Vixen Specifications

Mark	Powerplant	Span	Length	Height	Wing area
DH.110	Two 7,500lb thrust RR Avon RA7	50ft	52ft 1½in	10ft 9in	648sq ft
Sea Vixen FAW Mk 1	Two 10,000lb thrust RR Avon 208s	50ft	53ft 7in	11ft 6in	648sq ft
Sea Vixen FAW Mk 2	Two 10,000lb thrust RR Avon 208s	50ft	53ft 7in	11ft 6in	648sq ft

Mark	Empty wt	All-up wt	Max speed	Initial climb	Ceiling	Endurance
DH.110		35,000lb				
Sea Vixen FAW Mk 1			645mph		48,000ft	
Sea Vixen FAW Mk 2	31,715lb	45,700lb	640mph		48,000ft	3 hours

4 Production

Vampire Fighters

Prototypes:
   LZ548, LZ551 and MP838.

F Mk 1:
   TG274-315, TG328-355, TG370-448, VF265-283, VF300-334, English Electric-built, including F Mk 2s TG276 and TG280 and DH.108s TG283 and TG306.

F Mk 2:
   TX807.

F Mk 3:
   VF335-348, VG692-703, VT793-835, VT854-874, VV187-213, English Electric-built.

F Mk 20:
   VV136-165, English Electric-built for RN.

FB Mk 5:
   VV214-232, VV443-490, VV525-569, VV600-611, VV614-640, VV655-700, VV717-736, VX461-464, VX471-476, VX950-990, VZ105-155, VZ161-197, VZ206-241, VZ251-290, VZ300-359, English Electric-built.
   VZ808-840, de Havilland Hatfield-built.
   VZ841-852, VZ860-877, de Havilland Chester-built, WA101-150, WA159-208, WA215-264, WA271-320, WA329-348, WA355-403, WA411-460, WE830-849, WF578-579, WF584-586, WG838-847, English Electric-built.
   WG793-807, WG826-837, de Havilland Chester-built.

FB Mk 9:
   WG848-851, WG865-892, WG922-931, English Electric-built.
   WL493-518, WL547-587, WL602-616, WP990-999, WR102-111, WR114-158, WR171-215, WR230-268, WX200-226, de Havilland Chester-built.
   WG236-241, WX259-260, Fairey-built.

Exports
FB Mk 50   *Sweden:*
   70 aircraft 28101-28170.

FB Mk 6   *Switzerland:*
   4 F Mk 1s J-1001-1004.
   75 aircraft J-1005-1079 de Havilland-built.
   100 aircraft J-1101-1200 Swiss-built.
   3 aircraft J-1080-1082 Swiss-built.

F Mk 3   *Canada:*
   85 aircraft 17001-17087 less 17043 and 17045.

F Mk 30   *Australia:*
   57 aircraft.

FB Mk 31   *Australia:*
   23 aircraft.

FB Mk 5   *Norway:*
   4 evaluation+25 production aircraft.

FB Mk 52   *India:*
   39 de Havilland-built+247 licence-built.

FB Mk 5   *France:*
76 ex-RAF stock.

FB Mk 51   *France:*
183 licence-built Vampires.

Mistral   *France:*
250 built by SNCASE

FB Mk 5   *South Africa:*
10 aircraft+40 aircraft including FB Mk 9s.

FB Mk 5   *Italy:*
5 evaluation+de Havilland-built aircraft.
80 aircraft licence-built in Italy.

FB Mk 52   *Egypt:*
30 aircraft acquired from Italy and 20+ from
UK.

FB Mk 5   *Venezuela:*
30 aircraft.

FB Mk 52   *New Zealand:*
18 aircraft+8+20 ex-RAF FB Mk 5s

FB Mk 5   *Finland:*
6 aircraft.

FB Mk 5   *Iraq:*
12 aircraft.

FB Mk 52   *Lebanon:*
5 aircraft.

FB Mk 9   *Southern Rhodesia*
24 aircraft.

Vampire Night Fighters

Prototypes:
G-5-2, G-5-5/WP 256.

NF Mk 10:
WM232-256, WM659, WM730-733 de Havilland
Hatfield-built.
WM660-677, WM703-729, WV689-691
de Havilland Chester-built.

Exports
NF Mk 10   *Switzerland:*
1 aircraft J-1301.

NF Mk 10   *Egypt:*
15 aircraft (ex-RAF — cancelled) 1550-1564.

NF Mk 54   *Italy:*
14 aircraft (ex-RAF) 3.167-3.170, 3.211-3.220.

NF Mk 54   *India:*
30 aircraft (ex-RAF) ID592-609, ID1601-1612.

Vampire Trainer

Prototype:
G-5-7/WW456+Pre-production WW458 and
WW461.

T Mk 11:
WZ414-430, WZ446-478, WZ493-521, WZ544-
593, WZ607-620, XD375-405, XD424-463,
XD506-554, XD588-627, XE816-897, XE919-
961, XE975-998, XH264-278, XH292-330,
XH357-368, XJ771-776, XK582-590, XK623-637
for RAF.

T Mk 22:
XA100-131, XA152-172, XG742-777 for RN.

Exports
T Mk 33   *Australia:*
36 aircraft for RAAF.

T Mk 34   *Australia:*
5 aircraft for RAN+1 licence-built T.34A.

T Mk 35   *Australia:*
68 aircraft for RAAF built under licence.

T Mk 55   *New Zealand:*
6 aircraft NZ5701-5706.

T Mk 55   *South Africa:*
6+19 aircraft SA221-226, SA257-262, SA265-
277.

T Mk 55   *Norway:*
6 aircraft PX-E, PX-G, PX-M, ZK-X, ZK-Y,
ZK-Z.

T Mk 55   *Venezuela::*
6 aircraft 23-A-36, 2E-35 to 6E-35.

T Mk 55   *Portugal:*
2 aircraft P5801 and P5802.

T Mk 55   *Sweden:*
45 aircraft 28411-28455.

T Mk 55   *Switzerland:*
39 aircraft U-1201 to U-1239.

T Mk 55   *India:*
53 aircraft IY467-470, IY514-552, BY377-386.

T Mk 55   *Lebanon:*
4 aircraft L-151, L-154, L-159, L-160.

T Mk 55 *Iraq:*
7 aircraft 333-335, 367, 386-388.

T Mk 55 *Chile:*
6 aircraft J.01-J06+6 ex-RN T22s.

T Mk 55 *Finland:*
9 aircraft VT-1 to VT-9.

T Mk 55 *Burma:*
8 aircraft UB501-UB508.

T Mk 11 *Southern Rhodesia:*
12 aircraft ex-RAF.

T Mk 55 *Egypt:*
12 aircraft 1570-1581.

T Mk 55 *Indonesia:*
8 aircraft J-701 to J-708.

T Mk 55 *Japan:*
1 aircraft 63-5571.

T Mk 11 *Jordan:*
3 aircraft ex-RAF.

T Mk 55 *Ireland:*
6 aircraft 185-187, 191-193.

T Mk 55 *Ceylon:*
5 aircraft cancelled.

T Mk 55 *Syria:*
2 aircraft 493-494 cancelled.

T Mk 55 *Austria:*
8 aircraft including 5C-YA, 5C-YB, 5C-YC and 3 ex-RAF.

Venom Fighter Bombers
Prototypes:
VV612 and VV613.

FB Mk 1:
WE255-294, WE303-332, WE340-389, WE399-438, WE444-483, WK389-437, WK468-503 first 15 de Havilland Hatfield-built, majority of remainder de Havilland Chester-built, but some also assembled by Fairey and Marshalls. WL892-935, WL954-999 cancelled aircraft allocated to Bristol.
WR272-321, WR334-373 de Havilland Chester, Fairey and Marshalls-built.
WW669-710 cancelled aircraft allocated to Bristol.

FB Mk 4:
WR374-383, WR397-446, WR460-509, WR525-564 de Havilland Hatfield and Chester, Fairey and Marshalls-built.

Exports
FB Mk 50 *Italy:*
2 aircraft MM6153 and MM6154.

FB Mk 50 *Iraq:*
15 aircraft 352-366.

FB Mk 54 *Venezuela:*
22 aircraft 1A-34 to 8C-34.

FB Mk 1 *Switzerland:*
126 aircraft J-1501 to J-1625, J-1650.

FB Mk 1R *Switzerland:*
24 aircraft J-1626 to J-1649.

FB Mk 4 *Switzerland:*
100 aircraft J-1701 to J-1800.

Venom Night Fighters
Prototypes:
G-5-3/WP227 NF2, WV928 NF3.

NF Mk 2:
WL804-833, WL845-874, WR779-808, first 7 de Havilland Hatfield-built, remainder de Havilland Chester-built.

NF Mk 3:
WX785-810, WX837-886, WX903-949, WZ315-320 de Havilland Hatfield, Chester and Christchurch-built.

Exports
NF Mk 51 *Sweden:*
62 aircraft 33001-33062.

Sea Venoms
Prototypes:
WK376, WK379 and WK385 all FAW20, XA539 FAW21.

FAW Mk 20:
WM500-523, WM542-567.

FAW Mk 21:
WM568-577, WW137-154, WW186-225, WW261-298, XG606-638, XG653-680 built at de Havilland Christchurch and Chester.

FAW Mk 22:
XG681-702, XG721-737, all built at de Havilland Chester.

Exports

FAW Mk 53 *Australia:*
39 aircraft WZ893-911, WZ927-946 for RAN, all built at Christchurch.

Aquilon 20 *France:*
4 aircraft for French Navy, converted to Aquilon 204s.

Aquilon 201 *France:*
25 aircraft for French Navy.

Aquilon 202 *France:*
25 aircraft for French Navy.

Aquilon 203 *France:*
40 aircraft for French Navy.

DH.110

Prototypes:
WG236, WG240, XF828.

Sea Vixen

FAW Mk 1:
XJ474-494 (pre-production batch) XJ513-528, XJ556-586, XJ602-611, WN647-658, XN683-710 all de Havilland Christchurch-built + XP918 from de Havilland Chester.

FAW Mk 2:
XP919-925, XP953-959, XS576-590 all de Havilland Chester-built.

Below:
Eight FAW2s were allocated to ground training at RAF Halton having flown into Abingdon and then been moved by road. *Philip Birtles*

Bottom:
Sea Vixen FAWs XS577 was painted in the distinctive red and yellow U3 pilotless drone colours, but this programme of conversions ceased before any numbers were available due to budget restrictions. *Flight Refuelling*